READY, WILLING &
(unbeliev)ABLE

*Real Estate Agents'
Most Outrageous Stories*

Also known as: 101 Greatest Real Estate Stories Ever Told

A Reality Storybook by:
DONALD GORBACH

Handwritten note: Dear M, Couldn't - Can't - Wouldn't - Under any circumstances - Do it without you.... Merry Christmas

Copyright © 2011 Donald Gorbach
All rights reserved.

ISBN: 1466276916
ISBN 13: 9781466276918

Third Printing 2017
ISBN: 1503087204
ISBN 13: 9781503087200

SHORT TALES INSTEAD OF SHORT SALES!

I saw a FSBO sign that read: **God is our Lord and Realtor**

I saw a Real Estate For Sale ad in a local newspaper: **Spacious 2554 SF home with large lot, family room with fireplace, huge dick for entertaining and enjoying the view.**

I showed a house and there was a teenager sleeping in the bed in her underwear with no covers. She never woke up and never knew we had been there.

I saw a For Sale sign that said: **Must Sell! Neighbor's An A--hole!**

I read a "Handyman Special" advertisement with photo that captioned: **This home can be burned into an excellent investment.**

My sellers' dog escaped out the door when I was showing the property when they were not home. I took a raw pork chop from their refrigerator and chased the mutt down the street to woo it back again.

I had a client once who tied up two of his girlfriends in the house and set the house on fire. No one died but that was the end of my listing.

I once had a home inspector get bit in the rear end when the homeowner returned home and let his German shepherd out of the car.

I had a male client who had a sex change during our escrow. His name changed from Bob to Bobbie and he wore a mu-mu and heels to the closing.

A lady Realtor walked her clients to their car to bid them farewell. She closed the door for them - on her skirt. The car drove off taking the skirt with them.

A realtor friend of mine said he was leaving next week for Maine to help his sister get her house ready to put on the market. I asked, "To Bangor?" He said, "Get your head out of the gutter, she's my sister."

I saw an ad in the paper recently that said: **Oceanfront Home, 6,000 SF, Magnificent 6 BR, 6.5 BA, Courtyard Pool & Gazebo bar, Perfect for your Panties.**

CONTENTS

Dedication xi
Introduction 1
    Over The Edge 5
    It Could Happen To You 9
    When the Fat Lady Sings 12
    Palm Beach Sales Trifecta 15
    Shopping In The 5 & 10 17
    $1 Million Sale From $30 Lead 20
    The Qualified Buyer Machine 21
    Emergency Advice For Realtors 23
    Shut Up, Kid 25
    Believe In Yourself 28
    You're Fired! 30
    Good News…Bad News 33
    The Broker Was A Snake 35
    The Dream Home Was A Trash Heap 37
    Pays To Make A Good Impression 39
    Even Bad Impressions Can Work 42
    The Naked Agent - Not My Problem 45
    Mandatory Seller Disclosure 48
    To Tell Or Not To Tell 51
    Don't Worry, He'll Come Down 53
    Don't Judge A Client By Her Cover 55
    On Call 57

Dr. Looney Bin 59
Earth Wind And Liar 61
If It Seems Too Good To Be True 63
Married With Children 68
Money Down The Drain 70
Can You Facebook From Prison? 72
Nursemaid With A Realtor License 77
The Case Of The Bored Housewife 79
Commission Incentives Really Do Work! 80
The Most Revealing Showing 83
Blind Farming Can Get Into Deep Poop 86
Banking And Entering 89
Nice Try Squatter! 91
The Bite Of A Pit Bull 93
Like Father, Like Son 95
Cable Guy 98
The Don Knotts Of Real Estate 100
Little People 102
The Naked Bushwhacker 104
The Psychologist Needs A Psychiatrist 106
The Cabbage Patch Family 108
Frankly, My Dear 111
You Picked A Fine Time To Panic Lucille 113
The Gutsy Buyer 115
Nookie In The Pool 118
Clean Showing 121
A Little Misguided Faith Perhaps? 123

If It's Not Meant To Be, So Be It 125
Sentimental Seller 127
Wrong Exposure 129
Three's Company 131
Riding The Real Estate Coaster 133
The Perfect Storm 135
Warm Reception 138
Broker Caravan Blunder 141
No Time To Smell The Roses 143
Open House Stranger 145
My Open House Disaster 146
Cue The Deer 150
The Open House Viewing 152
It Was Quite A View 155
I Killed My Seller 157
The Price Was Right 161
The Sound Of Silence 163
The Spirit Of The Deal 165
Undaunted In North Las Vegas 167
Was It Something I Said? 168
Oh My! 170
Whips And Chains, Oh My! 172
A Lewd Encounter 174
We All Scream For Ice Cream 176
Amortized Over 100 Years? 177
Striking Oil 179
Ups And Downs 180

The Vanishing Listing 183

The Case Of The Disappearing Kitchen 185

Has Anyone Seen Our Garage? 188

Lost And Found 190

Circumstantial Evidence 192

Wrong Number 193

Why Do I Have To Sell My House? 195

Failure To Launch 197

Don't Shoot The Messenger 199

When It Rains, It Pours 201

It Was A Crashing Good Closing 204

My Sale Still Had Traction 207

The Cops Sealed My Deal 209

Persistence In The Face Of Adversity 211

Flea Flicker 214

Flea For All 216

The Unwelcomed Visitor 217

Business Went To The Dogs 219

The Runaway Dog 222

Nice Doggy 225

Dog House For Sale 227

Long Live Woman's Best Friend 230

Humane Being 232

Field Of Dreams 234

Pay It Forward 237

A Storybook Ending 240

The Curtain Rod: Fact or Fiction? 244
The Author's Story 246
Contributor List 248

To my brother Eric, I dedicate this book.

Thank you for the inspiration that turned my book dream into a reality.

There's not a day goes by that I don't think about you...

'twas heaven here with you.

Introduction

The Real World of Real Estate
Principles and Practices

From the time I built my first house at age six, my internal compass pointed me in the direction of real estate. Although that first construction project was just an industrious little boy's cardboard box house, my sails were set in a direction and I knew it even then. As described in my author's story, I then succeeded in the listing and sale of a house by the time I was twelve. Over the past thirty years, the mysterious winds of real estate have blown in many directions, but my compass has stayed steady. This book is about true real estate adventures. Some of the stories are from my personal Realtor experiences, but most are the tales of other real estate wayfarers traveling the roadways in search of buyers and sellers.

The beginning of my official real estate career, however, started when I enrolled in licensing school many years ago. They handed out a standard text book and the teacher began his lecture by explaining to the class that he would do his level best to make the coursework interesting. I took that as a tip-off of what to expect and I was right. Really, how fun does "Principles of Real Estate" sound? But the course was required for licensing so I studied the chapters on fair housing, contracts and closing, agency disclosure, license laws and broker relationships. The one and only really fun moment in that entire month was the day the instructor asked each student to tell what area of the market they were interested in pursuing. "After all," he announced, "you ALL can't sell million dollar homes." Most of them responded that they intended to sell within particular gated neighborhoods. Many aspired to specialize in golfing communities. Standing up and facing the class, I popped off saying, "Spend your time selling small beans if you like, I'll be the one selling million dollar homes and I don't care where they are." Everyone laughed at me, the standup comedian, but it was a self-fulfilling prophecy.

It has been years since that class and although I hardly remember a thing from the textbook, I do remember how boring the whole of it was. Later, when I closed my first transaction, I sent the instructor a note telling him of my first Realtor victory. It was an $11 Million transaction. What I did not tell him was that nothing in his principles course had a darn thing to do with how to **practice** those principles in the real world of real estate!

I can't blame the instructor for the lack of real life information in that textbook. For that fact, I can't blame my alma mater either for four years of boring textbook material. It is just the nature of this thing called academics.

I'm remembering as early as high school how we labeled some people "book smart." They were the ones who never studied much and always aced the tests. They seemed to know the text-book stuff inside and out with little effort. The others of us who struggled hours on end to keep up grades were said to have "street smarts." We street-smart types had a special confidence we would be successful in "real life" because we had common sense. We were savvy and had practical knowledge of why things existed and how to make them better. We saw little merit in relying on information found in schoolbooks, and besides most of that book information was just an exercise in short term memorization to pass a test anyway! Take the test and in a short term, every bit of the information was lost, permanently deleted from our minds. We learned from hands-on experience the know-how to survive in "real" life situations. Where this learning mentality comes from, I have no clue. It just was what it was and is what it is, a natural inclination found in us street smart types. When I was growing up, it was a great platform to stand on and worked every time whenever I had to explain why my @$B!Gt grades weren't quite the same as my book smart counterparts!

Under the theory that there are both street-smart people and book-smart people, I am proposing a learning approach that will work for both. It serves the best of both worlds. Since the real estate profession is my forte, that's the industry I am tackling in this book to prove my theory. This is "book smart" reading that provides "street smart" wisdom! I'm changing the world of academia here by creating the first "real book" of real estate principles AND practices. I've tried to create a story-telling method that will appeal to both seasoned veterans as well as newcomers in the industry. I've targeted the interests of home buyers and sellers too. These are true stories that expose real life experiences of licensed agents from all over the country. The stories present lessons that you will remember forever. Some are parables to ponder. You will also learn that in the "real" world of real estate, you must "expect the unexpected." I am not for sure, but I think Murphy's Law might have been inspired by the real estate industry with its simple universal truth, "What can go wrong, will."

This book could have easily been titled, "What They Never Taught You In Real Estate School, But Should Have." It is a collection of some of the best stories from my thirty year career in the business as well as from top agents in nearly every state of our country…from Maine to Hawaii. The stories have been chosen from thousands of submissions and we selected the ones here for their elements of surprise, inspiration and humor. Most of the stories submitted arrived in raw and unedited form. Thanks to my faithful editor, Katherine Margaret, the selected themes have been revised and enhanced, not only to protect the innocent but to pointedly accentuate the themes and keep the text uniform. Her proofing of the manuscripts, under my strict rules of compliance, required additional editing of offensive language, material not suitable for underage children and deletion of outright controversial political agendas. Oh yes, we also had to remove any expression of bias, discrimination, prejudice, slander or what you would generalize as any down-right crappy attitudes - which were too numerous to mention! It would appear that the hard times many of us are facing have caused some of our comrades to be less than jovial and, in fact, a little mean spirited. But not to worry because we have fixed that negativity, and I promise you it's all very good reading now...lol!

Under the theory that misery loves company, sit back and enjoy the book. It was written and compiled truly as a mission of love for the real estate industry, an industry that has been good to me for over thirty years and the 1.4 million licensed real estate agents everywhere, for whom I have the utmost respect.

Over The Edge

May 30, 2007, my cell phone rang at 8:30 a.m. For those who are not aware, real estate associates are on call 24/7, so this early morning call was not unusual. I looked at the LED and saw "Unknown Caller." I first thought to myself, "If they don't want me to know who is calling, why should I answer?" But, I took the call anyway out of curiosity.

"Hey, Jonathan, it's Sonny. How are you?"

Took a moment, then I made the connection who was calling and responded, "Good, Sonny. What's up?"

He replied, "You have a listing at The Slade on a high floor, right?" I answered affirmatively. "Well, I've been thinking about moving there since I have a lot of friends living in the building. Could you show me the unit at six this evening?" We agreed to meet same day at that time.

Over the past year, his face had become familiar in the local real estate circles. He would show up at developers' parties in West Palm Beach during showcase extravaganzas being hosted by different realtors. These social mixers were always well-attended by the "beautiful people." The pleasant evening bashes were generously funded with marketing dollars and included excellent catered services. With fancy appetizers, free-flowing booze and live entertainment, large crowds of people would show up. There was a lot of excitement over the rapidly appreciating real estate opportunities.

On one of those evenings, I was formally introduced to Sonny. The music was loud and the room packed with energetic socialites and business people. He was an outgoing guy, engaging everyone with his big smile. He and I chatted about real estate that night, chumming it up a bit as we circulated among other guests. By the end of the evening, we parted with the socially correct bidding, "We'll have to get together sometime."

During this period real estate was booming. Preconstruction sales were off the charts and many investors were flipping units to other buyers for a profit even before closing. The market was revving into high gear beyond all expectations. The builders' promotional weekend parties spilled into weeknights all over town. Most parties I attended, Sonny was there too and talking up a storm like the life of the party, laughing and joking. Whenever he and I conversed, it was strictly focused on real estate news; he never let it get personal. I assumed he had a broker of his own so I politely stayed away from any form of salesman overtures.

Over the next few months I continued bumping into Sonny, not only at the promotional parties but at mutual friends' house and dinner parties. He was always his same old jovial self. A true step-up-to-the-plate kind of guy. He would help the host with last minute tasks, bartending or running out for ice if needed. In all these occasions that we met and talked, I never found out exactly what he did or where he lived nor did I even know his last name. He managed to stay aloof in that area. I did take note that he often referenced "Palm Beach Society" and more than once had the feeling he was trying like a politician to win votes into the exclusive club.

A week before he called me to view my listing at The Slade Condominiums on North Flagler, I saw Sonny at one such social event.

It was the first time I had ever seen him accompanied by anyone. He introduced me to his lady friend. She was an extremely attractive woman and had been in the mortgage business for years. The three of us discussed a number of different condo projects. I gave her the full rundown on The Slade in the event Sonny or any other customer of hers might be interested in purchasing there. We exchanged business cards and went our separate ways. I never got a clear picture whether their relationship was personal or strictly a business relationship.

At four o'clock in the afternoon on May 30, 2007, I came home and told my wife I had a showing at The Slade at 6:00 p.m. and would be back shortly for dinner. But at 5:15 p.m. "Unknown Caller" showed up on my cell phone again and sure enough it was Sonny. He said his meeting had not lasted as long as he expected and asked if he could see the unit in the next ten minutes. Since I lived one building north of The Slade, I agreed to meet him right away.

Not ten minutes later Sonny walked into the lobby. I wondered what kind of meeting he had attended since he was dressed casually in shorts and a tee. Nevertheless, we greeted each other and I extended my right hand. He smiled and gave me his left as he was holding cell and car keys in his right. It was a clumsy moment between us and I sensed he was ruffled.

On the way up the elevator we exchanged small talk about the weather. The doors opened and we headed toward the unit. The Slade is set up in such a way that when you exit the elevator at the west end of the building, there is a considerable walk to the eastern most unit, the 01 line having the most magnificent views. As a matter of fact, I had once advertised this unit as "Incredible and Unobstructed Views of the Atlantic Ocean, Palm Beach, the Intracoastal and Empire State Building." When you look north from this unit, the Empire State Building is not much of a stretch!

On the way down the hallway, my cell phone rang. It was an associate at my firm so I took the call. I unlocked the door and told Sonny to go ahead and look around, assuring him I would be with him in a minute. I heard him drop his keys and cell phone on the kitchen counter and he hollered back at me, "Wow! This is really beautiful."

While still talking on my phone, I headed through the dining area to catch up with Sonny. I saw him open the sliding glass door and step out onto the eleventh story balcony. Before I realized what was happening, he was on top of the railing and I screamed, "Oh, my God! No! No!" But he disappeared over the edge. Sonny had jumped to his death.

Since that day, my life has never been the same.

Months later I was driving by the Slade with a new customer in my car. The client said, "Hey, there's the building that was in the news recently." Then asked, "What do you think the stress of that must have done to the poor agent who was there?"

I took a deep breath and answered, "Well, if it hasn't driven the poor guy over the edge too, it's likely this miserable real estate market could!"

It Could Happen To You

Recently I was sitting in a continuing education real estate class and the teacher shared an interesting story. He told it to be true and hoped it would serve in a motivational way for us to hear it. He made a disclaimer that he had no sales agenda whatsoever in telling the story. He even disavowed that any of his masterful teaching skills might have in any way influenced the outcome of the story.

Seems he had a twenty-one year old rookie student who had just earned his real estate license. The young man began working in the Jupiter area of Florida. The student, I am going to call him a "kid" since I am more than twice his age, landed his first listing only a few weeks after passing his licensing exam. It was for a rental on the grounds of an oceanfront estate. The little cottage had been built as a guest house and was privately tucked well away from view of the main house with its own driveway access.

The kid held a brokers' open house for his rental and several brokers and associates showed up for previewing. One gentleman, dressed quite smartly in an expensive silk suit, asked the kid if the owner of the estate would consider selling the whole place.

"I don't think so," replied the kid, "but I'll ask." The kid took the man's name and phone number with every intention of taking this possible buyer lead very seriously. As I am listening to the teacher's animated rendition of the story, I am thinking to myself, "Ha ha. That young kid has no idea what he is doing and there he is trying to play ball in the big leagues when he's still just a bat boy." I can think those kinds of judgmental and sarcastic thoughts when I am listening to people talk sometimes, you know?

But back to the story, the teacher went on to tell that shortly thereafter our rookie did approach the owner of the estate. The owner, whose rental had not yet been leased, responded to the inquiry with a rather glib retort, "For the right price, anything is for sale." But not to be daunted, the kid asks him to throw out a number and the owner smiles big saying, "Fifty million would work." Here I am thinking to myself again as I am hearing the story. "Ha ha. The owner knows the kid hasn't even rented the guest house out yet for him. So, he probably thinks, why not mess with the young whipper-snapper and throw him a little fantasy toy to chew on. Fifty Million Dollars."

Well, as the story goes, the kid calls up the man in the suit and tells him the price. The man calmly replies that he thinks the price is steep, but that he will discuss it with his client and get back with a response. One week later, the response came. The man tells the kid his client is interested and would like to see the home. The kid arranges the showing and the man arrives with his client.

Well, slap my condescending, I'm-twice-as-old-as-him attitude next door! The client ended up buying the whole estate for $43 Million according to the teacher. It was the kid's first transaction. And if that is not unbelievable enough, the man in the suit representing the buyer was actually the business manager of the client, not a licensed real estate agent, so the KID double-ended on the commission earning a whopping $2 Million on his first sale!

The teacher told how the rookie called him after the deal closed to thank him for the opportunity to become a millionaire. The teacher, quite savvy in the world of real estate, promptly asked, "Well, where's my teacher's referral fee?"

The moral of the story is this: Selling real estate is a piece of cake. (I just made that up.) The true moral of the story is that a big sale can happen to anyone. Being in the right place at the right time is sometimes all that is necessary. It could happen to you.

When the Fat Lady Sings

My first deal ever was a business op with land. It was a recreation center featuring mini-golf, arcade, go-karts, batting cages and located on approximately four acres of prime commercial property. My accountant had given me the referral. It was valued at $3.9 Million. And if you did not know, accountants are a terrific source for referral business. So to the drawing board I went on my maiden flight into big real estate business. Before meeting with the owner, a mentor agent in my office pointed out that my listing agreement should include a ten percent commission rather than the usual six. He explained that commercial listings are usually much harder to sell and I should try for the higher rate at my listing appointment.

The listing was signed with a ten percent commission and I went to work on trying to market the business and land. Since I knew it probably would not sell to anyone from the area, I decided to try a round of advertising in "The New York Times" and "The Wall Street Journal." It was a smart idea because I got more than fifty ad calls. I was able to schedule three showings in one day.

Two of those prospects seemed very interested and commenced to work on their due diligence investigations. About three weeks later I received my first offer, $3 Million. With some negotiating back and forth, a final agreement was struck between the buyer and seller. The agreed price was $3.5 Million. This twenty-one year old Realtor was counting his chickens! It was a mathematical snap for me to calculate the ten percent commission and I began writing my shopping list: oceanfront condo and a new BMW. What a business this is! Wahoo!

Closing was scheduled to be ninety days from effective date. Around three weeks before closing, the seller called to say we needed to meet. Okay, here it comes. I was fearfully anticipating his agenda might involve my commission and that he would try pressuring me to reduce it.

When I arrived at the center that afternoon to talk, I was greeted by the manager who sent me off to find the owner somewhere on the property. I found him sitting on a bench. He began to say he had a meeting with his family the night before and they all agreed he was too young to retire. This was not the right time to sell the business. I was speechless. To me, this was a bombshell of epic proportion. I was blindsided and could only respond by saying, "The buyer might sue." But fully prepared for this, he explained he had already talked with his attorney and was advised he had an "out" in the contract if he should choose to exercise it.

I was sick to my stomach. I thought I was going to heave as I walked back to my car in the parking lot, his parting comment still ringing in my ears, "Thanks, Don, and keep in touch." Those words seemed like an insult and as much as I wanted to go back and make nasty threats, I drove away. What a business this is!

Some six months later, I had moved on from the disappointment. My girlfriend called that day to remind me of our date the following weekend to attend the wedding of one of her friends. "I hate weddings," I whined, trying to wiggle out of it. "Come on, don't make me go." She reminded me I had promised. "Please don't make me go. It's an outdoor wedding. It's going to be 100 degrees. I won't know a single person there." But she was relentless in holding me to my commitment. That was that and next weekend there I was, attending the wedding from hell.

As the reception was winding down, a large and heavyset woman was singing with the band. Her voice was annoying me as I sat alone with my pouty self because there was no one I cared to talk to. A guy at the far end of the table piped up and asked, "Aren't you in the real estate business?" I affirmed with a nod and he went on, "I knew you looked familiar. I'm the manager of the amusement center you were trying to sell months ago. I don't know whether you've been in touch with my boss lately, but if not, you might want to call him soon. He's really been under a lot of pressure and not feeling that great." Truth was, I had put the painfully disappointing memory of that dreadful day out of mind completely as if it never happened.

However, the following day I pulled myself together and called the seller. When he asked me to come over to see him in the week, I jumped on the opportunity and we met that very afternoon.

Thirty days later, I was at the closing of my $3.5 Million sale! I did have to negotiate off my commission a little, but sure enough, I was able buy my oceanfront condo and new BMW. I learned a couple of valuable lessons that I continue to practice today. One, always listen to your woman because nine times out of ten she's probably right and will hold you to your promises. Two, never count your commission until you leave a closing with the check in hand. And third, even when the fat lady sings, it's not always over!

Palm Beach Sales Trifecta

When an agent in my office listed an $81.5 Million estate in Palm Beach, we were in the middle of the Bernie Madoff hedge fund catastrophe. The impact of his unraveling ponzi scheme was causing a lot of uncertainty in the markets. I thought because of this, the agent was going to have a tough time marketing and selling what was the most expensive residential property in town. As a matter of fact, it might have been the highest priced residential listing in the country at that time. I couldn't have been more wrong.

This magnificent property on five prime acres of Palm Beach oceanfront was "hot" from the minute it went on the market. It was owned by Jones Apparel's founder Sidney Kimmel. The amazing 32,000 square foot estate with three hundred feet of ocean frontage not only found a buyer immediately, but found several. There were multiple offers made on the home and it sold for full asking price. Even after it went under contract, another offer came in over asking price. Can it get any better than that? It can.

Two months later another Palm Beach agent sold a house down the road from the Kimmel estate. It was owned by George Lindemann, a Forbes 400 billionaire entrepreneur and major art collector. What was amazing about this was that the property was not even on the market for sale. The broker approached Mr. Lindemann with an unsolicited offer. Within days a deal was struck. The magnificent 27,000 square foot Polynesian estate was sold. Mr. Lindemann, who had no intention of selling his home, told the broker he had no choice, "It was an offer we couldn't refuse." The price: $68.5 Million.

Two of the highest sales in the country only two months apart in the same town, and in an economy that was going down faster than the Titanic. Can it get any better than this? They say three times a charm.

One month after the Lindemann sale, another Palm Beach agent got a call from one of her old customers who she had not dealt with in years. He was a Russian billionaire who was inquiring about a mansion that Donald Trump had bought years earlier in a foreclosure sale. Trump paid some $40 Million for it and spent another $20-25 Million in renovations. It was listed originally for $125 Million but reduced to $100 Million at the time of the Russian's inquiry. Another magnificent estate with 41,000 square feet and four hundred seventy-five feet of ocean front. Yes, completing the Palm Beach trifecta, this estate sold for $95 Million.

Three homes, three months apart for a grand total of nearly a quarter of a Billion dollars, and that is a capital "B" for Billion. In a real estate market that was floundering everywhere else in the country, these agents were highly successful. The moral of their story: timing is everything and being in the right place at the right time. Be ready because you never know where tomorrow may find you!

Shopping In The 5 & 10

Imagine doing Saturday floor time in your real estate office. You're working in the affluent town of Palm Beach, Florida when a good looking European couple walks in. The couple says they want to buy a home. They tell you they're looking for something on the island and need a minimum of three bedrooms in the $1

Million price range. Easy, right? That's just what happened to me last weekend.

I seated my new customers in the conference room and served them coffee. I logged onto our multiple listing website and my computer search confirmed what I already knew. There was not one home on the market in their price range. Can you believe it? For a million bucks, not one single family home on the island for sale.

If you didn't know, the island area of Palm Beach is known as a safe haven for the rich and famous. Celebrity types such as Rod Stewart, author James Patterson, Donald Trump, Ron Perlman and inmate Bernie Madoff have lived there, just to name a few. Before the collapse of the economy, the island had a bottom price point at $2 Million and as high as $100 Million. However, with the sagging real estate market even Palm Beach prices have been hurt, price points now dropping to $1.5 Million and on the high end, $83 Million.

Back to my clients waiting in the conference room. I explained to them that my search results showed no homes available on the island for less than $1.4 Million. Expecting some sort of dissension, I was surprised when they replied, "We were afraid of that." I asked them if they would consider a condo or even a terrific home in Manalapan which is also an affluent area, but they were adamant Palm Beach was the only place they would consider, so I went to work on my assignment.

Not one week after first meeting them, they put in an offer on a home listed for $1.5 Million. Even though the place needed a lot of work, it was only one block from the beach and located where prices are between $5 & $10 Million.

It's funny when you think about not having any homes to sell for a million dollars, and where else in the country would an agent with a million dollar customer go bargain shopping in the 5 & 10?

$1 Million Sale From $30 Lead

In 2004 I purchased a real estate internet lead for $30.00 which turned into a million dollar sale. The buyer lead was confirmed by email and explained that the husband had accepted a job offer as the new CEO for Ruth Chris Steak House. The family was now committed to relocating to New Orleans. I was their agent.

After showing them several homes in Metro New Orleans, they opted to buy a home in the exclusive Sanctuary Subdivision in Mandeville, a suburb of New Orleans. But shortly thereafter, Hurricane Katrina hit and Ruth Chris moved their headquarters to Orlando. My clients sold the home and moved there.

My $30.00 investment returned a $24,000 commission check!

The Qualified Buyer Machine

We have all been to an ATM machine to pull out a little cash when the banks are closed. In today's world, ATM banking has become a routine part of life. We take the money, retrieve our card and wait patiently for the receipt to print. With me, I am ready to snatch the printout the instant it rolls out. I would never walk away leaving it behind. Then I take a quick glance to verify both the withdrawal and balance in my account and tuck it away in my wallet with the money.

But imagine the look on someone's face when they glance at their receipt and discover it says: Available Balance $100,000,000. That is what happened to someone in East Hampton, New York recently. The poor guy had to pick himself up from the ground from a near heart attack until he realized the account number was not his. He has kept the prized receipt to show everyone he knows.

Can you imagine how arrogant a mogul you would have to be to grab your $400.00 cash withdrawal and walk away leaving a receipt behind that reflected an available balance of $99,864,731.94? Really! Would waiting another five seconds for the printout have just been way too inconvenient? Besides that, what kind of person would leave that much money in an account earning virtually no interest? But think about this, wouldn't this be a great lead for a real estate agent to track down? The ATM machine qualified him as a pretty high end buyer if he happened to be in the market for a home!

It just so turns out, the owner of the receipt had recently shelled out $43.5 Million, all cash, to purchase a mansion in nearby Sagaponack. The arrogant mogul then promptly demolished the home to build a new one more to his liking and twice as large. He was identified as a well known hedge fund manager, and obviously the dog days of yesterday didn't hurt him too badly in the pocketbook.

So I was thinking about several lessons learned from the arrogant mogul's ATM story. Oh, for sure, I will never put my $100,000,000 in a low yielding account like that, and I will definitely make certain to take my receipt so that no one will ever write a nasty story about me in the future. But most importantly, today I will be heading off to my nearest Palm Beach bank to do floor time next to the ATM machine!

Emergency Advice For Realtors

In August of 2003, I awoke about 2:45 a.m. with severe chest pains. I was taken by ambulance to the emergency room to be told I was having a heart attack.

> **Advice:** Never tell someone who is having a heart attack that they are having a heart attack. What are you trying to do? Give them a heart attack?

By 6:30 a.m. I had emergency angioplasty with a stint placed in my clogged heart artery, a routine procedure. I was feeling much better and placed in the cardio-intensive care unit at the hospital. The nurse came in to hook me up to the monitors and check on me. She looked to be in her early twenties and seemed to know what she was doing, so I relaxed.

> **Advice:** Never relax if you don't think your nurse knows what she is doing, especially when she looks very young.

While she went about her work, we chatted and I told her I was a Realtor. I asked if she rented or owned a home and she said she and her husband were in fact planning to buy a home as soon as he was finished with his classes in the spring. I apologized for not having a business card, after all I had arrived at the hospital in nothing but a t-shirt and my skivvies, but promised to get one for her. So next morning I had a friend bring some to me.

Two days later while walking the halls, still dressed in my open backdoor hospital gown, I found my nurse and handed her my card. I had a full recuperation and was soon back to work. Then some eight months later she did call, and I ended up representing the couple in purchasing their first home.

>**Advice:** Emergencies happen, but you should never leave home without your business cards - or your pants!

Shut Up, Kid

It was in 2005 and I'd just gotten my real estate license. I went to the real estate agent's training class that my broker sponsored for new agents. While sitting in class, I listened as the instructor explained that the average income for a Los Angeles family was around $40,000. Interestingly, the average cost of a home in LA at that time, which had been rising some 20% a year for the past five years, was around $450,000. Given the current interest rates, a couple wanting to buy had to be making at least $140,000 a year to qualify.

I stupidly raised my hand and asked, "Then why are sales going through the roof? If the average house costs over three times the average income, who's buying all these houses?"

The instructor waffled a bit and then quickly explained that three and five year ARM's together with stated income loans were fueling the buying market. Everyone knew that people would be able to refinance out of those loans at a later time once ongoing appreciation built equity in the properties and/or their income quadrupled in three to five years when the loans converted.

I was still having a hard time grasping the concept. From my experience, it seemed awfully optimistic to think that everyone should expect a 350% income increase in three to five years. Also, it seemed to me that if you did have an equity gain and refinanced, all you could do would be to change the terms of the loan, either the interest rate or number of years, and it still wouldn't help unless you had that 350% increase in income. Then, still trying to think it through, it seemed to me if you took equity out to pay the mortgage, you'd be increasing a loan amount that you couldn't afford to pay in the first place. Maybe the logic was that you could sell your house, capture the gain in equity and reinvest elsewhere? But, problem with that was all the other houses would have gone up in value too. Plus, I kept puzzling, if everyone tried to sell the homes that they couldn't afford in order to reap their equity, wouldn't that create a calamity in the market?

The whole thing just wasn't making sense to me so I asked, "Well, if we know that the market is this inflated and that in order to buy a house a buyer has to take on a loan bigger than they can afford in three to five years - unless their income goes up dramatically - are we agents working in the best fiduciary interests of our clients to sell them on these homes?"

One of our company higher-ups sitting in the class jumped in to respond, "Whoa, whoa there young fella. Sounds like you're trying to be a financial advisor instead of a real estate agent."

That's when I realized, holy crap, I'm supposed to go out there and cram people into houses at super-inflated prices that they can't afford even though I know it's more than likely going to destroy them financially? Are they telling me I'm supposed to go to my sphere of influence, my friends and my family and help them do something that I think is going to ruin them in three to five years, pretending it's alright just so long as I get my commission? All the old salts in that room knew this to be true. Whenever I asked them what they thought might happen when it all came tumbling down, they just shrugged, "Well, real estate has up and down cycles." Right, we all now know the last cycle has been equal to the great depression of the 1930's.

As for me since that class? I've never sold a single property. I hung around different offices until 2010 just to watch the disaster unfold and saw several brokers retire just before the collapse. Only one, a mortgage broker, ever admitted to me he knew that he was putting people into loans that were doomed from the start. His excuse was, "Well, if I didn't do it my competition down the street would have."

I always thought it funny he didn't choose my approach - go do something else. Today, realtors are still drinking the Kool-Aid and over the last four years still cramming people into homes that we all know are way overpriced when you consider the shadow inventory and artificially low interest rates. It's a cruel business and takes a special kind of person to stay in it keeping a good conscience.

Believe In Yourself

Cleveland Heights in the Buckeye State has many large old homes. Most are wood with three or four stories and full basements. They are classics from the late 1800's. The best of them have widow's walks on top, not something you see just everywhere these days. Many of the homes have been passed down in families from one generation to the next which accounts for why so few come on the market for sale. But one in particular was going to be sold and it was the home of Mr. Corley. He was older than dirt and a grumpy old man.

I met Mr. Corley first time during my listing appointment at his home. I knew ahead of time he was a widower, never had children and was ready to sell the place and move into smaller quarters elsewhere. I got the call to interview for the job after his doctor referred me to him. His doctor and I have been neighbors for years.

Following Mr. Corley into his parlor, we sat down and he proceeded to lay it out straight in a rant that excoriated every licensed real estate agent from here to Timbuktu. Taken aback with such a harsh tongue lashing right off the bat, I held my defenses to see if he was just testing my hide. Old guys do that sometimes. He went further in his tirade to tell me I was the third agent to come by and he unequivocally did not like real estate agents, matter of fact hated them all!

Landing that blow at me, I looked him dead straight in the eye and replied, "Well, Mr. Corley, I already don't like you."

With that, he cracked into a laugh and gave me the listing.

You're Fired!

People would say that I am a nice lady; I think it's true! I go about my work in real estate with every intention of providing professional service to the best of my ability. My work ethic is solid, and I am a person of good character. You can check my licensing and you will see my continuing education classes are up to date; I happen to be a stellar student, studying for the sake of gaining in real estate know-how.

With all that said, I think this story will show I still had some lessons to learn.

I was representing a seller who was a long time engineer by profession. His plan was to sell his townhome and buy a single family, detached house. He was attentive and detail-oriented during my listing presentation, reviewing the CMA closely. He signed the listing and I began my marketing campaign. His property was in perfect order, properly priced and I was confident it would sell quickly. We found the house he wanted to buy, however, he did not want to present his offer until he had an offer on his townhome.

An offer on his place did come in after about six weeks and to make the sell/buy transaction work I found myself faced with two problems: 1) My seller wanted a contingency stating he would not close escrow on his listed townhome until he closed on a replacement property, and a contingency that he would not close on the replacement house until his townhome closed escrow. 2) As to the replacement property, he wanted every kind of professional inspection known to man: sewer line, soils under the home, chimney, fireplace, mold, air quality, termite and more. He insisted the seller pay for all the inspections. As I tried to accomplish some of his requirements, it was becoming more apparent that I was dealing with an abusive bully.

He would call me at 11 p.m., grilling me over details and demanding that I make his buyer do this or do that, yelling at me to make the seller of his replacement house do this or that. At every turn, I was getting insulted and demeaned; the verbal abuse escalated to the point that I finally "fired" him as my client. I just could not take it any longer.

The lessons I learned from this horror story were: never accept bullying, always try to take control (preferably without making it obvious), continue to sharpen skills for handling difficult people and get further education in property physical conditions. I will admit, I can now better recognize problems like when a yard slopes down toward a neighbor's property and might cause flooding issues between adjacent properties, the need for ventilation and vapor barriers in crawl spaces to prevent mold, sewer lines from house to street that need photos and many other conditions that can affect the desirability and value of a home. This bully client did his research like no other.

Although he was the worst client I ever encountered, the additional real estate training I received while working with him really taught me a lot. But I fired the bully anyway!

Good News...Bad News

I recently showed a million dollar condo to a former client. He showed lukewarm interest, so I told him there was another unit that had just come on the market and it would be a much better investment. It was on a golf course with tremendous views of the ocean from every room. I explained it had the best location, being the northeast corner of the building with wraparound balcony providing both sunrise and sunset panoramas. Not wanting to waste his time or mine, he asked if I had seen the property. I told him I had - which was true. He asked if I could sell his place for a profit. I told him I could - which was also true.

Next day I scheduled the appointment to show him this great condo. It was in a complex with three separate buildings. However when I pulled up, I realized the unit I thought we were going to see wasn't the same one that had just come on the market and, quite the opposite, was located on a southeast corner with no golf course view and only miles of empty beach to look at.

Greeting my client in the lobby, I knew I had to spring into action. I announced that I had good news and bad news. The bad news was that we were not going to view the unit I originally told him about; the good news was that we were going to see a better one! He planted his feet and crossed his arms, then asked me whether this "better one" had northeast views of the golf course. I told him no, and with a thumbs down gesture grunted, "You don't want to be on the golf course." He was stumped by this and asked, "Why not?"

"Too dark!" I went into overdrive.

I told him he'd never want to be facing north no matter what the view; it would be dark all day long. Not sure whether he should swallow that one, he asked, "But I thought you told me that the golf course view was the most desirable?" To which I promptly said he had heard me wrong, that in fact a SOUTH-east corner would be more desirable than anything, adding, "You should know that!"

"Does this one have a wraparound balcony so I can watch the sunsets?" he questioned. I shook my head and pointed out that sunsets here on the East Coast are not so spectacular. In fact, it is the sunrises that are most prized. After a pause, he looked at me with a half-cocked grin and said, "I've never met a bigger BS'er in my entire life!" He was completely disarmed at this point and went on to say since I had always steered him in the right direction in the past, and he happened to like me, he would go see the unit. He loved it and bought it.

After the closing, he wrote my broker a letter telling him he had "the best BS'er in the business working for him!" My broker felt it necessary to read the letter aloud at our weekly office meeting and now there's hardly a day that someone doesn't ask me if I have anything in a northeast corner.

My advice: You'd best have a positive history with your client before using this sales approach!

The Broker Was A Snake

There was a broker who sold a lovely five bedroom home to a nice family. The home was located on nearly two pastoral acres in a rural area. The price was just under $180,000. The family who bought it had two small boys and the wife was pregnant, a third child on the way. They had heard some town rumors that the home was priced low because there was a snake infestation, but the broker assured them that the "snake story" had been invented by the previous owners in order to get out of their mortgage.

When the couple closed on the house, they signed a document from the bank that disclosed the property may have snakes. Seems that in spite of the couple making numerous visits to the property during the escrow, no snakes were ever seen so they felt the snake rumors were contrived.

As spring arrived, however, the family began to discover that there was an infestation of snakes. As a matter of fact, there were hundreds of snakes showing up. They were garter snakes, a small, harmless type of striped reptile. The children could not play in the yard because of them. They slithered constantly across the driveway and onto the front porch. But worse than this was the invasion of snakes into the house. They would slip behind the walls at night and inhabited the well, releasing a foul smelling musk that tainted the drinking water.

The husband put up a battle and once killed forty-two snakes in a single day. He had a routine of performing a "morning sweep" through the house while his family slept. He would rap a stick against the ceiling and could hear dozens of snakes scatter. Once he removed panes of vinyl siding and dozens dropped out. He even made his way through the crawl space under the house and found snakes everywhere.

Turns out that the house was believed to be built on top of a snake den where large numbers of the reptiles gathered to hibernate during the cold winter months. It was also found out later that the couple who bought the house prior sued their seller, as well as the real estate agent involved in the transaction over the same snake problem. The locals had been referring to the property as the "snake house" over many years for good reason.

Finally, the family couldn't live under these conditions any longer and moved out, a day after their new baby daughter was born. They had no recourse against the bank since they had signed the disclosure. They stopped making payments and the bank foreclosed. The couple filed bankruptcy.

This nice family has never been the same since the fiasco. Do you have any thoughts on what should be done to the real estate broker who sold them the house?

The Dream Home Was A Trash Heap

Life was good and after years in a professional and lucrative career, the time had come to buy the home of their dreams. This is the fabulous fantasy of everyone and for some, it becomes a reality. For Stan and his wife, their dream home in Florida had become true. It was a magnificent property, fulfilling their every wish but for one thing, a swimming pool.

Now that they had moved in, Stan and Nora consulted with their contractor, an architect and a landscape designer. A swimming pool of impressive design was to be built in the backyard as the finishing touch for their exquisite dream home. After all these years, the happy couple's fantasy would soon be completely materialized.

When the bulldozer began clearing away dirt in the backyard, mountains of trash began emerging from the dig site. There were tires, washing machines, metal parts and even a lawn mower being unearthed by the dozer. At every step, there was more trash being shoveled up from the fifteen foot deep excavation. This was beginning to look like a serious problem; their house had been built on top of an old trash heap.

Who was liable for the problem? Was there a broker who failed to provide disclosure? Do you think Stan and Nora were ever able to complete their fantasy dream home with pool? Would they have to settle for an above ground pool? Only time holds the answers to those questions, but they could look at their situation on the bright side, the house could have been built over a snake pit!

Pays To Make A Good Impression

I had two incidents in the past year that could have landed me in the local jail if not for my professional appearance. Innocent as could be, I found myself in circumstances that appeared incriminating and criminal. Both times, if not for my professional look, I would have been cuffed and thrown in the back seat of a police car. I tell you, it pays to make a good impression!

The first incident happened when I showed up for a broker's open house. I arrived at the last minute, and as I opened the door to the townhouse thought it strange nobody was there. I walked in and several times called out a hello, but the place was deserted. There were no brochures, no agents in sight and no sign-in sheet. But since I was there, thought I might as well preview the property. I looked through the living and dining areas, the kitchen and even the outdoor loggia and pool area. Then I went up the beautiful stairway and meandered through the bedrooms with my last stop in the master. Knowing most of my clients are interested in large walk-in closets, I was delighted to find his and her matching wardrobes with custom cabinetry. This was very impressive.

Startling me from behind, a woman suddenly appeared in the room. She barked, "CAN I help you?"

I had no idea who she was, so I introduced myself and politely responded by saying that I had seen everything, then added a few compliments about the lovely house. While squinting suspiciously at me, she wryly answered, "What are you doing in my house?"

"Well I'm here for the broker's open."

Still quite indignant, she stated, "There's no open house here. My house is not for sale. I don't know how you got in here and you need to leave."

Though perplexed by her statement, I complied and started heading toward the front door, all the while trying to explain there must have been a mix up with the information I had. I handed her my business card and after looking it over, she seemed to calm down. She then began to tell me she was about ready to call the police when she heard someone upstairs. However, when she saw a brand new BMW parked in her driveway sensed it might be safe to investigate for herself first. She said she really didn't think a burglar would have driven up in a new foreign sports car and when she peeked in and saw I was wearing a business suit, decided not to 911 her cell. We ended up having a good laugh over the incident and she accepted my apology for the mistaken intrusion. As I was leaving, I told her if she ever decided to sell, just give me a call. I promised I would come next time by invitation only. She chuckled and said it was a possibility.

Turns out the townhouse that was open for brokers was further up the street. I missed the viewing of that one, but all was not lost because I had met a new prospect. Who knows, I could end up listing her townhouse some day!

The other incident occurred several months later. It happened at my client's home. Their property was a magnificent oceanfront estate that I had sold them some five years earlier. My clients were out of town and had received a call from their security company because the house alarm had gone off. There had been a bad rain storm that morning causing the electricity to go out in the area and that no doubt had caused the power surge which tripped the system. I was on their backup emergency phone list since I lived nearby, so when the clients phoned me about the security call, I told them I'd be happy to go by and check the house.

As I drove up to the front entry gate, I pressed the four digit code in the keypad but nothing happened. I did it again and still the gates wouldn't open, so I parked my car, took off my suit jacket and proceeded to climb over the front yard wall. Talk about going above and beyond the call of duty for clients!

Making it over the wall, I walked around checking doors and windows to make sure everything was status quo. I investigated the back of the house and the pool area as well. Everything was fine.

Now to get back to my car, I had to go over that wall again. It was about five feet high and a foot or so wide, not easy to climb. I laid over the top on my belly, threw my legs around and started to back down, feet first, to the other side. Just about then a man shouted, "Can I give you a hand?"

Caught by surprise, I looked about. There was a police officer waiting. I gulped and smiled like the Cheshire cat! He showed no sense of humor at all. He just stood silently like a concrete statue, arms crossed, feet apart. Once on the ground, I started some fast talking to explain myself because it looked like I was about to be in some big trouble from the look on his face. There was a long pause…finally, he relaxed his stance and said, "Okay. When I saw the new BMW in front of the gate I knew there was no crime being committed here." He let me go.

My second arrest averted.

It sure pays to make a good impression!

Even Bad Impressions Can Work

The year was 1979. The place was Cottage Grove, Oregon, a town of about six thousand residents and located twenty miles south of Eugene. I was employed at Grove Realty along with twelve other agents. This was one of the two largest offices in town. When I got my license in 1976, I never intended to sell real estate. I just wanted to learn about real estate and thought going to school and getting the license was the way to go about it.

At that time in my life I had $8,000 in the bank and my wife had a job. I thought I was a pretty wealthy hippy. Then I figured since I was licensed, I might as well hang legitimately with a real brokerage; maybe a deal would fall in my lap every now and then. A strange thing happened. For whatever reason, people seemed to really like me, and I became one of the top agents in the office within my second year.

My real estate car was a second hand 1969 Ford Econoline van, not exactly what you would think of as a plush transport for clients. My wife and I lived less than a hundred yards from my office so it was a commute that made my life convenient, especially because I was remodeling our 1890 vintage Victorian cottage which I worked on when I wasn't doing real estate. I am a self-taught professional know-it-all remodeler without a contractor's license of course, never wanted one either. I just do it my way without the book.

Even Bad Impressions Can Work

One morning I got up and decided it was time to take our month's supply of garbage to the dump. I am cheap; I am not paying the city for trash pickup so I load it up and start for the dump. Now understanding that I have what you call self-diagnosed ADD, I am thinking I should first stop by the office for a cup of coffee and donut with my associates. But no sooner did I walk in the door when the receptionist shouts, "Carl, why are you dressed like that? You are supposed to be on floor duty!" I hate floor duty. Everyone knows I constantly try to pawn it off, but I screwed up on the schedule and didn't get a fill-in for myself that morning. So there I was in my "go to the dump" clothes and had to excuse myself to run home to change into my "floor duty" clothes, my one and only leisure suit.

Back to the office I go hoping that no one shows up during my stint. Not to be so. A nicely dressed middle aged woman came in wanting information. Her husband had applied for a job and if he got it, they were planning on moving to Cottage Grove. We went into the conference room and I told her all the groovy things about our little town. When I finished, I offered to give her a little tour around town and a drive by of some homes. She thought that was a wonderful idea.

We headed out to my hippie van where it had been roasting in the hot sun for several hours. I had forgotten that the van was loaded with what was now some very ripe garbage. The minute I opened the door, it was pretty noticeable but I put my client in the passenger seat anyway and reached into my pocket for my van keys to get us moving down the road, but no keys. I realized I had left them in my dump clothes laying on the floor at my house a hundred yards away.

Did I tell you the garbage in the van smelled a lot? It was hot. I didn't have the keys, and my nicely dressed new client was sitting there. I did what any normal self-respecting Realtor would do.

I said, "I'll be right back!" I dashed home and returned to find that she was still waiting for me. Wow! I started my stinking van up and gave her the best forty-five minute tour of Cottage Grove in my deluxe garbage truck anyone could imagine.

Three months later, guess who came into our office asking for me? That nicely dressed lady and her husband were there to buy a home in Cottage Grove and that is just what happened.

The moral of my story is: Forget about your fancy car! Smelly vans work just as well.

The Naked Agent – Not My Problem

I am a licensed real estate professional who has worked in the Malibu area for many years. My clientele are very wealthy people who live the LA lifestyle to its fullest and consider themselves entitled to the finest amenities money can buy, especially when it comes to oceanfront homes. Let there be no mistake, the value of oceanfront real estate is exorbitant in Malibu. It represents status and is a source of great pride for those who can afford to buy there. This type of client is picky, sometimes difficult to handle and always critically discerning. Catering to their whims can be challenging, but I have learned over the years that it simply comes with the territory.

Several years ago I had been working with a new client who was looking for a Malibu oceanfront estate. Her criteria was set in stone as it pertained to certain minimum standards regarding square footage and number of bedrooms and baths. Given the limited inventory of oceanfront properties in Malibu, meeting this strict criterion meant it could take many months while waiting for that just right property to come on the market. After showing her only six properties over the course of eight months, I worried she was losing faith in me as her agent and becoming discouraged.

Then a fellow associate called to tell me about a pocket listing he had just taken. The Malibu listing sounded perfect for my client and I quickly arranged for a preview of the home. The associate met me at the property and I could not have been more delighted in what I saw. The price was great, condition perfect, the style and square footage matched my Malibu client's requirements as did number of bedrooms and baths. Beyond that, the elevation of the view decks was an engineering masterpiece. It was a very desirable property. I was convinced this was going to have to be a fast and perfect showing to my client before any competition came on the scene.

Leaving the preview, I thanked the associate for letting me in on his pocket listing. He could have kept it to himself for a round trip had he wanted, but he explained that he was having personal problems and just needed to get a transaction closed quickly as possible. He further mentioned that his wife of many years had filed for divorce, leaving him in a bad way. Not my problem, but condolences to him for his bad fortune. I was merrily on my way back to the office to call my buyer client to set the appointment to show. Eight p.m. next night would be the perfect time to see the sunset from this gorgeous property. I was setting the stage for the perfect introduction of what I hoped to be my client's new home.

As the estate was vacant, I asked the agent if I could go by the home ahead of time to make sure there was not so much as a fingerprint on the oceanview windows. Everything would have to be just perfect to make that all-important first impression on her. He gave permission and apologized for his personal issues getting in his way of taking care of these details. Not my problem; I was in my "lead, follow or get out of the way" mode on this sale, and I arrived the next morning to polish everything with perfection, decking the place with flower arrangements to impress my buyer. All was ready for me to walk my client in the front door at sunset that night.

About middle of the afternoon, I received a bothersome call from the listing agent. He seemed to be drunk and was calling to wish me luck on the showing that evening. I pretty much cut him short. Not my problem. I was on a focus here and at 8 p.m. pulled up to the Malibu mansion with my lovely client. She was very excited to see the home, and I let her know what good fortune it was in finding this rare, pocket listing. I was selling this house to her as hard as I knew how!

Key in the door, anticipating the glorious moment of her first peek, I faked a drum-roll for drama and flung the huge, double doors open. What was supposed to be the perfect first impression was met with the shock of a naked listing agent leaned over the balcony rail, staring out to sea like a drunken sailor with his bare, white butt facing right at us. "Oh!" was what came out of my client's mouth. And when the drunk naked fool turned around, my client screamed even louder, "Oh, oh, oh!" There he was in all his naked glory, full frontal view with privates hanging like a droopy noodle on center stage! Clothes strewn across the floor and empty whiskey bottles, the place was a mess. What I had thought was NOT MY PROBLEM showed up at my showing as a potentially deal breaking problem.

The final chapter of the story is good though in that my client did end up buying the house. The agent got his commission and has taken a sabbatical leave from Malibu real estate sales for the time being. As for me, I will be much more careful about flippantly thinking, "Not my problem."

Mandatory Seller Disclosure

It all started with a call from an old friend of mine. He told me he needed to find a home and would like to be settled before Christmas. Having known this gentleman for years, I was excited and said, "That's great, I promise we'll get you and the family in so your wife has plenty of time to bake Christmas cookies!"

"No, I don't think so, Randy. I recently found out my wife was having an affair so she is out of the picture. We're getting a divorce. The house is just for the kids and me."

Of course I was saddened by the news and pledged my undivided attention to the matter. I dove into my research mode right away as I knew he was anxious. Christmas was three months away, and he hoped to make the transition quickly for the sake of his children. So we began house hunting.

He had outlined for me all the details pertinent to his requirements in a home and pressed hard on the idea that it also had to be a property that could close quickly. We viewed several vacant properties and found the perfect home in less than a week.

Before writing my client's offer, I spoke with the listing agent. He explained that the home belonged to a couple who were going through a divorce. Both the husband and wife had already moved out, but since their court date was three months away, closing on the sale would not be possible until then. He suggested that my buyer rent the now vacant home and close the deal once the court affirmed the sale.

After showing the home to my friend's children and getting their happy approval, my buyer wrote his offer and it was accepted. I instructed him thoroughly on the issue of renting before closing and he was delighted to proceed with the plan. He and his children would be moving into their rental home in two weeks with the closing on the sale as soon as court approval was granted.

When the first paperwork on the rental and sale began to circulate, there was a most unusual discovery. The seller's agent phoned me. He explained that his seller-wife was not certain if anyone else realized the odd situation going on. I, of course, asked the agent what was that? I was uncomfortable for a moment that some sort of impropriety in the transaction was being inferred. The sellers' agent then told me that the house my client was renting, and under contract to buy, is owned by one and the same man who had the affair with my client's wife. Yes, the seller-wife knew of her husband's affair with my client's wife. What was the chance of this coincidence happening? I had to sit with this information for a few minutes.

Not half an hour later my buyer phoned me. He said he had been reviewing all the paperwork and had just become privy to some information about the owners of the home. I interrupted him and said I might have just received the same memo from the listing agent. My buyer confirmed it. The situation was looking sticky by my way of thinking and I immediately told my client I could get him out of the deal.

With the biggest belly laugh I have ever heard, he said, "What are you talking about? I am staying put in the deal. I am getting a great house and he is getting a cheating witch!"

Now just where would you enter this kind of information in the seller's disclosure?

To Tell Or Not To Tell

One of my girlfriends has been a really good source of referrals over the years. She recently referred one of her former boyfriends who wanted to buy a home. Although she broke up with him fifteen years ago, he has remained her friend and every year he is included on the invitation list to her annual Christmas party. He faithfully attends, never missing one. That is where I first met him. He is still a single guy even after all these years and has an excellent career in law enforcement. It is obvious he continues to have a little crush on her.

He called me to discuss his house wish list and explained he was in no hurry to buy. His requirements were clearly defined and typical for his price range. Problem was that he was open to a very large geographic area around Orange County. This meant there would be many properties that matched his parameters. He requested I email listings to him and adamant that he wanted to do only drive-by's; he would do that on his own. Week after week I emailed listings, and week after week there were none he wanted to view. After six months, he called to say he found the house he wanted.

I was really excited at long last to show him a house! He explained it was a vacant home, he had looked in the windows, walked around the yard and that was the property he wanted. He would meet me at my office to write up his offer next day. Wow! Talk about an independent guy. My curiosity was killing me to know which house he had chosen after such a long shopping time, and he replied, "The one on Silvia Street, that's the one I want to buy." And he did.

After his transaction closed, I handed my girlfriend a little gift for the referral and she was of course happy it worked out for me to get the deal. "What did he buy?" she asked, and I gave her a brief overview of the property, but I am still not sure if I should tell my friend Sylvia his new address on Silvia Street!

Don't Worry, He'll Come Down

About twenty-five years ago, my parents found a property that they loved in the town of Westport, Connecticut. Mom was especially smitten with it. And I, even as a young high school boy at the time, fell head over heals in the fantasy of living there. It was really perfect, handsomely laid out over five acres of prime oceanfront property in the most prestigious area of Westport. The mini-estate had a huge pool with massively kept lawn overlooking Long Island Sound. There was a separate guest house privately set on two manicured acres of land, all graced with hedges and stately trees of various sorts. Being there made me feel like a young aristocrat.

The agent who was showing my family this magnificent property stated the asking price was $850,000. That was a very hefty sum of money back then. Mom advised dad that we just had to have this property because it was the most unbelievable piece of real estate she had ever seen. So dad, who always listened to her, instructed the agent to write up an offer for $750,000. The agent presented his offer and the owner countered back $800,000 firm. Mom insisted at that point dad go up in price. Reluctantly at first, he finally went back at $775,000, not a penny higher. The broker presented the new offer, but the owner was steadfast, $800,000.

Dad, who was a real estate agent himself, put the brakes on at $775,000. Mom pushed as hard as she could at that point insisting he should not blow the deal over the $25,000 difference. Dad confidently assured her the owner wouldn't want to blow it either over the difference. "Don't worry, he'll come down." But, my fantasy was not to come true, a new buyer showed up and bought the property for $800,000. It was sold to someone else that quick.

Several years ago mom read about that same property selling for $12 Million, not including the guest house and two acres! Understand, my parents have been married for almost sixty years now; they have developed a good read on each other over the years, and mom knows exactly the choice moments to rib dad about the "one that got away" twenty-five years ago. Maybe you have let one get away too in the past, but I bet it wasn't a $12 Million one!

Don't Judge A Client By Her Cover

I was doing floor time one day and a customer walked in. She looked disheveled, drove an older vehicle and was drastically over weight. Trying not to let myself make a rash judgment, I asked her a few questions. Okay, I confess, I had already made a rash judgment before asking the questions. She explained that she was going through a divorce and needed to find her own place now. She was interested in looking at condos because without a husband she could not take care of house maintenance and yard care. I had no interest whatsoever in getting involved in this victimized woman's drama.

Now, as it turned out that day, there just so happened to be a newly licensed agent in the office who I knew to be eager for work. I decided, from pure generosity of heart of course, that this delightful customer might be great training for our office novice. I spoke to him about the customer, and he was more than enthusiastic to take the opportunity. He even offered to split the commission or give me a referral fee if he closed a transaction with her, but I heartily declined. I figured if this customer ever did buy something, it would be such a small sale that dividing up the commission would just make me look greedy. Boy, what a stupid move that was.

Twenty-five days later the novice salesman closed an $850,000 oceanfront condo for the woman. Seems she was married to a very successful restaurateur who had made a swift and generous divorce settlement with her. She had carte blanche to buy whatever suited her. I got nothing! Not only did I not get the $50,000 commission but lost out on a referral fee of around $10,000. I promise you, I will never judge a client by appearances again nor should we ever judge a book by its cover, right? I think they taught us that in kindergarten.

On Call

Years ago when I was selling real estate, I had a fellow Realtor who was a very pretty blond. She had a cold call while on floor duty and made an appointment with the gentleman to show a $53,000 home. She arranged to meet him on a specific corner near the hotel where he was staying, and from there she would drive him to the property. He was a business manager who was going to be permanently transferred to our city by a well-known restaurant chain.

She drove up to the curb in her nice white Jaguar where a man dressed in business attire was standing. Putting her passenger window down, she immediately smiled, greeting him with, "It's nice to meet you, hop in and let's get going."

The man leaned in the window and asked, "How much?" to which she quickly replied, "Maybe $52,000."

"My god, woman, what are you selling?" he retorted.

"Well, it's just a little two bedroom house. Are you David?" she asked.

With that, the guy nervously glanced up and down the street, then laughed and said, "No. I thought you were a call girl."

She quickly pulled away from the curb, and after driving around the block came back to the same corner where she was more careful to pick up the right man. The other guy was nowhere in sight.

Dr. Looney Bin

One of our seasoned agents who has been with the brokerage firm for twenty-five years received a phone call from a prospective buyer. The buyer said he had received information about one of her listings from a co-worker at the hospital and was interested in scheduling an appointment to view the home. This agent primarily deals with high end properties and has represented many medical professionals over the years, so this call was not outside the usual network of her clientele.

The buyer explained that he was in residence and stuck there 24/7 so it would be best for her to meet with him at the hospital. She agreed, confirming the day, time and place of their appointment. Professional agents know the importance of providing first class, personal service for their wealthy clients, and her professionalism ranked with the best of them. Mapping out directions to the hospital, she prepared herself for a polished presentation upon meeting with her new client.

When she arrived at the hospital, the security gates at the entrance of the parking lot struck her as a bit unusual, but not to be daunted, she quickly phoned the client who gave her the gate access code in order that she could park her car. No problem. Upon entering the main doors, she was greeted by a receptionist. She explained that she was there to meet with Dr. Tima and that he was meeting her in the cafeteria. Saying nothing, the receptionist tipped her head inquisitively and pointed in the direction of the cafeteria. At the end of the hallway, our agent could see the cafeteria through a wall of windows, however, the dining area looked empty.

Fortunately, standing next to the doorway of the cafeteria was a male nurse. The nurse asked for the name of the person she was coming to visit. Again, our agent identified herself and with whom she had come to visit. The male nurse politely asked her to wait at the door, then returned a few minutes later with a doctor.

Wishing to make a terrific first impression on her new doctor client, our agent graciously extended both hands as a warm greeting. Beaming with the confidence of a successful business professional, she introduced herself, then pushed right into suggesting they sit down for their meeting. After all, showing leadership enthusiasm is important in real estate sales and she was passionately ready to lead this client to a house buying victory!

Oddly, the doctor seemed completely unmoved with her overtures, then cleared his throat and hit her with a little bombshell of clarifying information. The Dr. Tima she had come to meet was actually a long-term patient at the hospital who was currently undergoing extensive psychotherapy. Further, he explained that Mr. Tima was under the protection of conservatorship authority and certainly not legally able to purchase a house.

We all had a great laugh when our agent returned to the office with this story. It was true that her new doctor client was in residence; she learned he was also a resident!

Earth Wind And Liar

Sitting at the front desk in my office on floor duty one day, I watched as a big, black limo pulled up. It was a stretch-limo, so long as a matter of fact that it had to park diagonally in three spaces to be out of the traffic lane. The staging for this arrival screamed, "Notice me! I'm here!"

I watched the chauffeur open the passenger door. The middle-aged man came in and introduced himself by name, extending his hand. Offering my usual handshake and Realtor greeting, he abruptly cut me off in mid-sentence, adding, "I'm the drummer for Earth Wind and Fire." Whoa! Now he really had my attention. He was a famous musician and rock star!

He said he was interested buying in the Monterey Bay area and most especially Carmel. We sat down together and began reviewing properties that might fit his requirements. He suggested we go to a local pub to review the listings and have a beer, so with printouts in hand, we loaded into his limo. This sort of social entertaining in real estate is of course necessary to form trusting business relationships and since this client was going to be a big spender, I was totally on board. Our meeting was casual and lively. The client chummed it up with the waitresses and even wrote a little song for the gals. He was a big hit with those ladies, and I will admit I was pretty impressed with his ad-lib performance too.

Plans were made to begin viewing properties, and several days later, we were on our way traveling in my car up the coast. We visited four fabulous estates that day. The famous drummer then asked me to head on up to San Francisco to his finance manager's office. He was ready to make an offer and needed to pick up an earnest money check. The property he chose had a $4 Million price tag. After more than an hour's drive, we finally arrived in the financial district of downtown San Francisco where he directed me to a particular building. I parked and he went into the building - never to be seen again!

After waiting way too long, I went into the building looking for him, looking for any office that could be a finance manager, booking agent, rock band office or law firm. Gone like the wind he was, and I realized I had just been used by a con man and a liar.

It turned out he was a robber, working the whole northern coast from LA to Washington. He eventually got caught and arrested for grand larceny. His specialty was breaking and entering expensive homes. He was also found guilty of dozens of petty thefts in the Oregon area. The real band, Earth Wind & Fire, was notified of the impersonator and the police investigation was finally laid to rest. The publicity of the story did serve as a good warning to real estate agents to beware of con artists using realtors to gain access into homes.

Fellow agents, take heed from my lesson,! You just cannot believe everyone in the world today nor should you judge a person by the clothes they wear or the car they drive. Remember my experience with Earth Wind and LIAR!

If It Seems Too Good To Be True

I was a newly minted Realtor in receipt of my license only a couple of weeks when three men walked into the Century 21 office where I worked. Two of them were big, hulking, un-smiling security types fitted with wired earpieces snaking out from their collars. Both had not-so-subtle bulges under their jackets that were probably some serious guns. I gulped and tried to act nonchalant as if this stuff happened in the office everyday. Through the plate glass window, I could see another burly secret-agent sort leaning against a black Mercedes limo with two Dobermans inside.

The third guy in the lobby was smaller, nattily dressed in slacks and a sport coat...with no visible lumps beneath it and he did all the talking.

"My name is Rick. I'm in town for forty-eight hours," he said, "and I want to buy a large and private home with as much natural security as possible. I'd like a water view, garage space for at least six cars and no visible neighbors. Price is not an issue and I'll be paying cash. Is there anything you can show me today?"

"Um, sure," I stammered, doing my pathetic best to appear unimpressed.

While the trio waited in the lobby, I went back to my desk to see what might be available that would fit at least some of his parameters.

"Well, there is really only one property available now that might work for you, but...it's priced at 4.7 million," I tell him. The two bodyguards showed no reaction at all, their expressions were flat and in fact, they looked bored.

"That's not a problem," Rick replies. "If the house suits our needs, then we'll pay full price. I don't like negotiating." And he looked directly in my eyes when he said it.

"Right, me either." I mumble.

So I phone the Realtor representing the seller and schedule an appointment for us all to meet at the estate's front gate in an hour.

"You'll ride with us," Rick says. I felt my stomach tightening in knots at the thought of getting into that limo, but something told me not to argue. I could see the headline in tomorrow's paper, "Realtor's Bullet-Ridden Body Found Dumped in Bay."

As I'm walking toward the car I'm calculating the enormous commission I'll make on this, my first Real Estate deal. As soon as the driver opened the door, both dogs leapt to attention with fangs bared. In that moment, my whole young life flashed before me, but those commission dollars flashed there too and I got in before common sense could rear its ugly head.

On the way over to the property I try to make polite conversation by asking about the stupidest question imaginable. "So Rick... what do you do for a living?"

For the first time, I notice the two silent bodyguards crack the faintest of smiles. "I work for the government," says Rick. "But I can't tell you anything more. I'm sure you understand."

When we arrive at the estate, the other Realtor is already there waiting.

I introduce Rick to the Realtor who smiles warmly and shakes his hand. The two goons stand back behind the limo silently surveying the surrounding hills and the bay below. Now they're talking in hushed tones into their suit jackets. I watch her eyes widen as she takes in this scene, but she plays it cool.

The agent takes us through the property, first showing us the main house, then the caretaker's cottage, the fully equipped gym, the pool house, a putting green and we finish with the tennis courts. The seller, it turns out, is an international art dealer and the house is filled with priceless, irreplaceable work. My eyes are popping but Rick and his entourage have nothing to say until we've left the house and we're back in the limo. For about half a second I think about petting one of those dogs, but I don't want to ruin a promising afternoon in the emergency room, so I sit on my hands.

"Jon," he says, "you've done a great job. That's exactly what we want. Write it up at full price, and as I mentioned, we'll be paying cash. No contingencies, no inspections. I want it to close as soon as possible. I'll meet you tomorrow morning at ten o'clock with a deposit."

Once back at my office I'm giddy with excitement and I regale my fellow agents with the unfolding story. The seasoned pros looked skeptical, but I ignored that. I knew what I had in the palm of my hand here and I wasn't about to let anyone stifle my joy. I mean, I recognize jealousy when I see it.

READY, WILLING & (unbeliev)ABLE

The next morning the same group showed up promptly at ten, just as he said they would. This time the two bodyguards waited in the parking lot while Rick signed the offer and handed me a leather briefcase.

"What's this?" I ask.

Rick smiles and opens the case, revealing $180,000 in stacks of banded one hundred dollar bills. "You need a deposit, right? Well, here it is. Go make the deal," he says, "and I'll phone you tomorrow at ten."

Now my head is spinning and I'm feeling almost drunk with success. I phone the other agent, meet with her to hand off the paperwork, open escrow on the property and then I call my girlfriend. "Let's go out for an amazing dinner...anywhere you like," I say. "Don't worry about the cost. In fact, go out and buy yourself a new outfit and maybe some good jewelry to go with it."

Then, on a whim, I stop at the Mercedes dealer on my way home. I pick out a new black SL and write a non-refundable deposit check for a thousand to hold it until escrow closes in three weeks. I don't think there is anything in the world that smells better than the fresh leather seats in a brand new, about-to-be-mine Benz.

That night at dinner, my newly bejeweled girlfriend and I make plans to travel to Hawaii as soon as the deal closes. In fact, just to impress her, I phoned the travel agent from the restaurant, paying for the airline tickets and hotel on my credit card. I think we also discussed buying a little house together too. I had a lot to drink that evening and I don't remember everything we said, but in that moment, life was good.

At 4:15AM the following morning the phone jangled next to my bed. "Jon, this is Rick," the disembodied voice spoke. "I'm afraid I won't be able to complete this purchase. I'm in jail. Please do whatever you can to get my deposit back." He probably didn't mean that last request to sound like a threat, but to me...it did. I lay there in the dark figuring out how much money I had spent over the past 24 hours...money I didn't actually have of course, and never would.

The morning's paper had the whole story splashed on the front page. "Major Drug Kingpin Arrested in Tiburon." As it turned out, the seller of the property saw the headline too and I guess he realized the wisdom of quickly releasing Rick's deposit, just like I did.

In the end, I was left with only the sweet memory of those leather seats in that black SL that I wouldn't be driving anytime soon.

Well, that and one hell of a story.

Married With Children

I had been working with an out of town client for several months. I was diligent to keep Ron informed as new properties came on the market in the area he was interested, always talking to him but had yet to meet his wife. Finally, he brought his wife with him to town and we spent two days looking at houses. There was one that they seemed very interested in, but for whatever reason, Ron did not want to sign a contract.

I gave him a follow-up call the day after he and his wife left, but was told Ron's father was in the hospital. With all due respect, I decided not to crowd him. As a Realtor, when you've got a fish on the line you know you'd better reel it in pretty soon or lose it, right? And to add more pressure on me, there was a $2,500 bonus on that particular deal but only for two weeks. The clock was ticking and I waited another three days before calling him again. I explained that the newly constructed home was now completed and move-in ready, so it would likely be sold to someone else quickly if he didn't take action immediately. He said his father had passed away and it would be another week before he could even think about buying a house.

He called me back the following Monday, continuing to show an interest in buying but by then the house we looked at was already under contract. We kept in touch over the next two weeks when I noticed the house was back on the market, the buyers couldn't get their financing.

To me, this was a "hurry up" moment. I needed to get in touch with Ron ASAP to let him know he had a chance again for the home. I called his cell and left a message. I also called his home number and a woman answered. I asked for Ron and the woman replied, "This is his wife, can I help you?"

"Oh, hello, Sue. This is Jason Turner, how are you?"

Her reply was a flat response, "This is Pam. Who is Sue?"

I quickly hung up and dialed Ron's cell again, leaving a call back message there. Later that day he returned my call and seriously began reprimanding me, "I told you to **always** call my cell phone!!"

Yes, it turns out the woman Ron came to town with was not his wife. Due to my call, Pam did some investigating on her own and guess what? Ron and his wife ended up in divorce court and I had busted my own deal.

Money Down The Drain

It was a gorgeous Saturday morning in May 1984. I was alone at the Century 21 office where I worked as an agent. This was a good time to catch up on my never ending pile of paperwork, my least favorite thing in the world to do. Getting out on my boat today was my motivation to finish as quickly as possible.

A woman who was visibly distraught walked in and asked to speak to my broker right away. I apologetically explained that Neil did not come on Saturdays and I had no way of contacting him. On the verge of tears, she dramatized that her rent was overdue and wanted to tell him in person what had happened. This tenant seemed terrified that she and her children would get evicted. She used big hand gestures as she spoke and was nervously animated. She proceeded to tell me her story of woe.

Seems she had counted out all of her rent money which was $495.00. There were four hundred dollar bills, four twenties, a ten and a five that she had set in a neat stack on her coffee table, all ready to bring over. She left the room and when she returned discovered all of the money was gone! She buried her face in her hands and began to sob as she continued. She said she was in shock when she realized that her three year old son had flushed all the money down the toilet. She didn't know what she was going to do now.

I have no idea what came over me in that moment, but I leaned back in my chair crossing my arms over my head in relaxed fashion. With a straight face I said, "Don't worry, ma'am, everything is okay because you're lucky here. See we have a plumber who specializes in just this type of thing. David has a high-tech, special machine that he puts down the pipe. It makes a beeping sound when it detects money, sort of like a Geiger counter, you know? Then all he has to do is dig down, open up the pipe and retrieve the money. He even washes and dries it so it's good as new."

The woman stared at me incredulously for a moment. Her eyes were fixed on me and mouth slightly open as if she was not believing her good fortune. "Really?"

"Oh, yes, we use him all the time. I'll call him right now," and I swiveled around to the phone. Well, glory be, I guess she couldn't take the heat because she started sobbing again and confessed that her whole story was not true.

To this day I don't know how or where I ever came up with such a BS story on the spur of the moment. I do know this though, my story topped hers!

Can You Facebook From Prison?

I have been a Realtor in Tennessee for over fifteen years and my career has been very successful. Prior to working in the real estate industry I owned a consulting company specializing in comprehensive staff development within the medical profession. In that, I worked with private practice physicians. Not only did I make recommendations in the areas of office systems and procedures, but also hiring, firing and training of staff. I have good experience in making judgment calls when it comes to people.

One day while on floor duty, I had a walk-in client named Bob. There was nothing unusual about his appearance or demeanor. He was affable, self-confident and presented himself as a professional businessman. He explained that he had a corporate office in Florida and was in the restaurant business in five different states. He told that he had recently leased a suite in a local strip mall for his administrative office in Tennessee. I looked his business card over and recognized the street address. What he needed me to do involved two different things. One was to represent him in the purchase of three single family homes that were for his key employees who would be transferring to the Nashville area. The second assignment was to help him locate and buy a restaurant business. The houses needed to be ten day escrows and would be all cash deals; he detailed price point and particulars as a guideline. All of this work was of an urgent nature as he was very busy and had strict timelines in meeting his business expansion goals.

With a handshake, he left me with several phone numbers of his employees and asked that I get with them immediately to start looking for the right homes.

Over the next two days I did meet and show houses to two of his people. One was his secretary-treasurer and the other his business manager; they gave me their business cards. The decision was quickly made to write offers on three homes. When Bob and three of his key employees arrived at my office, I was surprised that the three were signing the offers instead of Bob, not to be a corporate purchase as originally stated, but I wrote the contracts as instructed. All three properties were quickly negotiated and went into escrow. His secretary-treasurer then scheduled home inspections on all three of the properties, normal due diligence on the part of a buyer in this area.

Something was starting to smell a little fishy to me though. The earnest deposit checks from "corporate" had not yet arrived at the escrow office for the three homes. The payment to the home inspectors was to be coming from "corporate" as well. I finally asked Bob for the number of corporate in Florida and talked to the manager there. I was relieved when she assured me all the checks were in the mail.

Next day I was meeting with Bob at my office to go look at a restaurant that was for sale. He arrived on time and I drove him to the business. The restaurant owner talked with Bob for over an hour discussing in detail the business' financials, inventory, vendors, menu and so forth, things that any experienced restaurant buyer would need to know. Everything was looking positive for a deal to be put together and later that day, believe it or not, a contract was signed by both the buyer and seller, all cash with a ten day close.

Still, something was nagging my gut about the whole thing. The secretary-treasurer was a pretty rough looking lady both in appearance and behavior. It just did not seem to fit that someone like that would be holding such a high level job. The business manager was about twenty-five years old and similarly did not look the part. As a matter of fact, had I met that kid on the street I might have thought him to be a punk gang banger. I decided to do a little super-snooping.

I drove to the business suite address listed on Bob's card. There in the strip mall I saw a vacant storefront and a "For Rent" sign in the window. My nerves were getting rattled again, so I did a smart thing. I called the leasing agent listed on the sign. He confirmed that the suite had in fact been leased by Bob. He was waiting for a check from Bob's corporate office before handing over keys.

My mind was being torn between what appeared to be legitimate and what did not seem to match up in small ways. I had just put in seven days of full time work trying to make my real estate assignment come together, but there was still no money from corporate. My escrow officer called to ask me about the earnest checks and we began to talk about our concerns over the legitimacy of this Bob guy and his band of so-called employees. I checked again with his manager in Florida. She stated the checks had just been returned to her due to an error in addressing the envelopes. She could wire funds directly to escrow if I got the routing code for her, which I agreed to do. The leasing agent at the business suite still did not have a deposit check. The home inspectors had been told same string-it-out story. It was time for me to get to the bottom of this troubling situation since closing on the three houses was only two days away. The pressure was building.

As agent representing the three individual house buyers as well as Bob in his restaurant purchase, I was in the middle of volumes of paperwork. There were title people, several different escrow companies, home inspectors, title reps and of course four different listing agents for me to juggle. With so many people involved, I decided to get some legal advice before taking one more step. I went in and met with the owner of the title company handling the transactions. I knew him to be both an attorney and a pretty savvy title investigator. I expressed my vague, but nagging sense that something seemed wrong, giving him as much detail as possible about the situation. He told me to sit tight; he would do a little checking on the Bob guy and get back to me quickly.

Next morning I received a phone call from the Tennessee Bureau of Investigation. Oh, my gosh! They wanted to meet with me at my office, and an hour later I was face-to-face with three TBI agents. They told me they were working on a case that involved Bob and would need my assistance. They would not explain exactly what their interest in Bob was about but needed me to set up an appointment with him so that one of their undercover people could make an identification. Of course I would cooperate with them.

I phoned Bob to tell him that he and I would have to make a final walk thru of the three houses before closing on the deals next day. Restaurant closing was also moved up to close that day…at Bob's request. We met at one of the houses and the undercover agent posed as my real estate assistant. I had Bob sign the final walk thru forms and reminded him again about the money for closing next day. He acted annoyed, but told me to "just get him" the routing number for the title company and he would see to it himself that the funds were wired next morning. For my next act I should have been awarded an Oscar because I smiled, shook his hand and showed so much excitement for him as he left that day

AS IF he was really going to close on these deals. He just couldn't thank me enough for the excellent job I had done.

I never saw or heard from Bob or any of his employees again, except once nearly two years later. The TBI later told me that Bob had been in prison years ago. While there, he befriended his "secretary-treasurer" by mail who became his girlfriend, and then-accomplice once he was out of the pen. The business manager kid had been a guard at the prison who Bob manipulated into joining the con game as well when Bob got released. In fact, Bob had blazed a trail over five different states in the past six years with the same con game. His ultimate con was in getting the routing number of title companies, then somehow stealing money from them through a wiring process. Yes, my clients were gone, no checks ever showed up anywhere and the poor home inspectors got bilked out of their pay.

In the end, I was never told whether they apprehended Bob and his gang or whether the crooks had slipped through TBI's fingers and disappeared. It made me nervous for a while not knowing, and I was left to unravel all the entanglements of those real estate contracts. After explaining to everyone what had occurred with the TBI, the contractual matters got resolved with no legal consequences for me. Thank goodness!

In my own defense, my instincts were right when I sensed something was fishy. My mistake was in not taking my instincts more seriously in the beginning. You sure live and learn in this business! But, my story is not over. Two years after I so cheerfully bid Bob goodbye at our final walk thru that day, I got a "Friend Request" on Facebook from him!

Nursemaid With
A Realtor License

A client, I'll call her Lacey, fired her other agent and hired me. She said her previous Realtor was unresponsive. In due time, I would find out what kind of response attention she was expecting.

At the end of our first month, I reviewed my cell phone bill and counted one hundred eleven incoming calls from her cell number. Lacey's home phone and work phone calls put the icing on the cake in my thinking. I was going to have to pull the reins in on this high maintenance client.

Believe me when I say, I am a high energy, service-oriented Realtor who will go the extra mile every time for a client. I am a tenured Realtor with a terrific repeat business to prove my claim, but I do have my limits and Lacey crossed the line with me.

One day when she was out of town, Lacey phoned to ask if I would go by her home to check on her teenage daughter. Since it was my listing, I rationalized it to be in my best interests to preview the home before a scheduled showing by another Realtor that afternoon. After all, I understood most teenagers might not keep things as tidy as should be.

Tidy was not the problem, however. Lacey went on to explain she wanted me to check on her daughter to see, and I quote, "if her chicken pox had completely cleared up yet." I found out later that Lacey had also put me on the emergency contact list for all of her children!

The Case Of The Bored Housewife

I was still in my maiden month as a licensed Realtor. I did a home show by myself and was happy to meet a couple who were looking for a house. Being quite proud to have my first client, I poured myself into providing the best service possible.

I started taking the wife out several times a week to look at homes. Each time, she and her two young children would meet me at my office for the tour. Being helpful as could be, I took care of transferring the kids car seats from her vehicle into the back seat of mine. I was diligent to keep the air conditioning at a comfortable level for mom and her little ones, even provided bottled water each time on our excursions.

After about three weeks and somewhere between twenty and thirty viewings with the wife, I finally got in touch with the husband one evening on their home phone. Just as I began to tell him about one particular home I thought would be perfect for them, he interrupted and said, "We already bought a home and will be closing on it next week."

Apparently the bored housewife just liked me and I had been providing entertainment for her and the kids!

Commission Incentives Really Do Work!

Over the past thirty-five years in real estate, I have had the good fortune of enjoying hundreds of wonderful experiences relating to listings, sales, closings and commissions. I consider it a privilege to have worked with so many quality people along the way. Every experience has touched me its own unique way, but there was one experience that is a most memorable one to tell. It was when I listed and sold a Gentleman's Club. It was literally a most touching event, tongue in cheek, when it happened many years ago.

Now for those who do not know what a Gentleman's Club is, the phrase is a fancy way of referring to a strip club. For you commercial real estate people, I am not talking about strip as in shopping mall. This was a take-the-clothes-off-and-dance kind of strip.

I had recently made a big sale in the area that had been well advertised and because of this, the owner of this fine establishment contacted me. I dropped everything and went to meet with him promptly. He, Big John who casually went by BJ, wanted to sell both the property and business. His plan was to move South and needed to sell the club to get on with that plan. Although I had no idea how to formulate a value for this sort of business, BJ did. I established the property value and put the two numbers together for an agreed listing price of $1.5 Million. He signed the

Commission Incentives Really Do Work!

paperwork. As an additional incentive to get his club sold, Big John told me there would be something extra for me if I sold it within ninety days. To me, there was no need for any incentive once the listing was signed, but heck it never hurts. I figured he would pay me a cash bonus of some sort. After all, his was a cash business.

I started marketing the club and chose the "New York Times" business opportunities section for my advertising. It was a great source for buyer leads from all over the country, and I began showing the business steadily to prospects, most of whom were businessmen with similar enterprises. The tours were always during daytime hours, and I did my level best in presenting it, but the club really sold itself. It was well run, had a good reputation and had been recently remodeled. It went under contract within thirty days. What a homerun for my smart and successful young self as I double-ended the deal. The closing was set for thirty-five days later.

On the day of closing, BJ invited me to stop by the club for a little celebration later that evening. I did and we did! It was sometime in the wee morning hours that BJ walked me out to my car which had been parked in his private back entrance area, and we made our jolly farewell. When I got into my unlocked car to leave, lo and behold! There was a most gorgeous girl sitting in my passenger seat smiling at me like she wanted to become my new best friend. She introduced herself as Tiffany and handed me an envelope with an airline ticket in it. She explained that we were going on vacation together the following week, leaving Wednesday. I don't know how all the details stuck in my head, but they did. This was to be an all expense paid trip to the Bahamas with Tiffany escorting me, compliments of BJ. He had kept his word about giving me something extra. Wow! Talk about the ultimate blind date and the ultimate incentive package.

Had I known in the beginning this was the incentive bonus, who knows I might have sold that place on day one! The blind date to the Bahamas with Tiffany went down as one of my best vacations ever. Trust me, I have been around the world, but never like this!

P.S. Well, bust my bubble! A week after the vacation I found out that Tiffany was not her real name.

The Most Revealing Showing

On a Saturday afternoon a few years ago, I was excited to take Sophia and Dan, potential home buyers, to view some properties. I had confirmed showing details for several homes in the hilly section of Sherman Oaks, California. Sherman Oaks is in the San Fernando Valley section of Los Angeles.

When we arrived at our last stop that sunny afternoon, a vacant home, the Realtor was not at the security entrance to meet us. However, the electronic gate was open so I parked at the street and we proceeded to walk up the long driveway toward the vacant home. The driveway was lined on both sides with tall shrubs, creating a privacy wall in front of the home. At the end of the driveway were a number of parked cars. They were exotic cars, the very expensive kind. "Odd," I thought to myself, "but maybe the owner is a car collector and stores them here."

Passing by the cars and rounding the wall of hedges, the house came into full view. The three of us froze in our tracks as we tried to digest a most unexpected sight. Momentarily stunned, we were looking through the huge picture windows into a grand room that was filled with naked people. I lifted my sunglasses to make sure I was not seeing an illusion. I blinked at least twice to make certain, but sure enough there were fifteen to twenty men and women busying around in the buff as if it were a regular cocktail party. The place looked buzzing with chatter and animated laughter. Double-D boobs were everywhere! In real estate language I might have said, "Great curb appeal," but what I was staring at was definitely called great "curve" appeal. Big-haired blondes with golden-tanned skin popped out even more noticeably when a well-built guy passed by them. He glided by like a handsome swan crossing Swan Lake. The large, open room was a Hollywood film set. There were cameras, spot lights, electric cords running everywhere and some ornate pieces of furniture staged in the room.

Yes, we had walked into a porn shoot.

To the left of the house was a manicured garden and several outside crew people looked our direction. I sensed they were especially eyeing my client Sophia who just happened to be gorgeous, statuesque and blonde. Her husband, Dan, standing about a half head shorter than her must have looked to them like he could have been Sophia's manager.

As we stood there still feeling a bit stupified by the unexpected sight, a woman approached and extended her hand to welcome us. I stammered in my embarrassment, but choked out a response to inform her I was a Realtor, there to show the house to my clients. She asked us to wait for her to check with someone in the house. While we waited, Dan caught the attention of a naked starlet inside who began waiving at him. Sophia mused along by pushing Dan forward as if she was encouraging him to go in the house. Dan and Sophia played it up well. The woman returned just about then, but sheepishly declined our request as it was just not a good time. Sweetly she added, "You can come back later for another viewing if you'd like."

With great restraint until we were well down the driveway, we then burst out laughing. Dan poked at me in jest insisting I had failed to bring popcorn for the show. Sophia chimed in that I should inform her of the dress code next time so she could arrive more suitably attired. We all agreed it had to be the most revealing showing in California history. And, by the way, we did not go back for a second viewing!

Blind Farming Can Get Into Deep Poop

As a new agent, I was trying to farm in the county's geographic information computer system for vacant lots and land. I ran across a six acre parcel with an out of state owner. As beginner's luck would have it, I found a phone number for the owner and got him on the line.

I introduced myself and asked if he was interested in selling. He was a sweet and very religious old man. He said that since I called him out of the blue (heavens), it must be a sign that it was time for him to let the property go. He explained that he inherited the property from his late wife of forty years. She had been given the parcel way back in the 1950's. He knew the property to have road frontage on two sides with sewer and water and that it was in a good location, though he had never actually seen it. I used the tax value for pricing and faxed a listing agreement to his local copy store where he signed and faxed it back that same evening. Made that listing look quick and easy, didn't I?

Next day I drove way out in the county to put my sign up and look the acreage over. Oh sad and disappointing site! My beginner's luck was looking more like a crummy prank as I realized my easily-begotten listing was the abandoned sewage treatment plant for Camp Davis, an old World War II military base. The place had eighteen ground level concrete ponds, slew troughs and huge round sediment tanks. Anything that might have ever been of any value was stripped and gone. What on earth was I going to do with this?

Research! And that's just what I began to do. I found out that after the government had abandoned the treatment facility, it was sold to a man who farmed frogs. He stretched chicken wire over the ponds and then threw scraps from a local meat processing plant on top. When maggots formed in the decaying meat, they would eventually fall through the wire and become excellent food for the frogs. Lovely, huh? I think the FDA has since outlawed that kind of frog farming business.

Brainstorm! That's what I did next. I called the local university to get in touch with the Department of Marine Fisheries. I hoped they might be interested in purchasing my listing for a hatchery. No interest whatsoever. Then I called the Army and Marine Corps base to see if they would clean the place up since it was formerly a military site. Wouldn't touch it with a ten-foot pole.

I was beginning to see that I was going to need someone with vision, someone who could see the…um…potential this property had. After a few months and some good advertising, I did find that person and, acting as dual agent, put a contract together and had the closing attorney start the title work.

Unfortunately, his title work opened a can of worms. Since the owner had not probated his deceased wife's estate fifteen years earlier, the attorney had to file and then formally close her estate in court. Next, the description on the land was so out of date the attorney required a new legal description to assure title coverage. How do you get a new legal description? Pay for a survey! And $6,000 later we had that pesty problem solved. However, a bigger infestation of challenges was yet to emerge. The nine page quit claim deed had to be signed and notarized by every heir of the deceased wife; the fourteen heirs were scattered across ten different states, with one granddaughter who was homeless and nowhere to be found.

In conclusion, I have two things to say after going through that twelve month long struggle. First, we did close the deal and it was the most interesting transaction I have had in the past ten years. Secondly, I learned a very important lesson: Beware of blind farming - you can run your tractor into some deep poop!

Banking And Entering

I deal with foreclosures and was assigned a property on Rutgers Avenue, but the bank neglected to tell me there was a north and south Rutgers Avenue. Of course I went to the wrong address. When I arrived there on Friday morning, I looked in the windows and not seeing much in the way of valuable furnishings or trash, assumed I was at the correct home.

Later that afternoon, I met my locksmith at the property so that he could change the locks. I took the necessary photos and went back to my office to prepare my BPO. In short order, the paperwork was complete and I faxed the listing agreement package to the bank. Next morning, I returned to put my sign in the yard, lockbox on the door and inputted the listing into the computer with confidential remarks to agents that the home was scheduled for clean out and could not be shown until the following Monday. My clean out crew was lined up for 1 p.m. on that day.

Early Monday morning my manager got a call from the owner wanting to know who changed his locks and put a sign in his yard showing the house for sale. He couldn't get in his home. What a call to get from my broker first thing on a Monday!

After talking to the bank, the confusion got cleared up quickly and I was able to meet with the owner and hand him a new key. He was really pretty pleasant about the ordeal, saying, "At least I got a new lock out of the mix-up!"

I shutter to think what a major problem there would have been if he had not come home until Tuesday because his house would have been completely cleaned out.

Footnote: The correct house was actually in better shape than his.

Nice Try Squatter!

Up in Oregon, REO properties have been quite the commodity over several years. This story is just one that stands out in my memory. It challenged my real estate courage to new heights!

I had just been assigned a new REO listing. The house had been vacated, but there were remnants of a garage sale still inside when I went over to change the locks and put my For Sale sign up. The prior tenant contacted me to collect the rest of her belongings, so I agreed to meet her there the following day when I was also meeting the contractor, roofer and trash crew at the property.

Next day, I had just pulled into the driveway and parked when a large U-Haul truck came backing up the long drive toward the house. I walked down the middle of the pavement waving my hands for the truck to stop, but the driver leaned out the window and yelled, "Get out of the way or I'll run you over." I stood my ground. He stopped and got out of his truck in a huff and I could see trouble was coming! Marching toward me, he insisted he had a lease and was moving in. He told me to get the h--- out of his way because he was in a hurry.

"No, you're not moving in this house," I stated emphatically. "It's not for rent."

He became even more belligerent and again threatened to run me over if I didn't get out of his way, but I continued to stand my ground as he stomped back to the truck and started it up. Quickly calling my client, I confirmed there was no mistake about any rental and then dialed 911 for assistance. Just about then my contractor and roofer pulled around the truck and parked, quickly realizing there was a problem brewing. The trash crew of two more people pulled in and parked in front of the U-Haul. Then the prior tenant pulled in followed by the previous owner and his posse. It was beginning to look like a riot.

I recognized the previous owner as a familiar face in real estate. He was a lender. Apparently, he figured if he moved his friend into the house, it would buy him a little more time to hold onto his already foreclosed home and collect some rent money! The truck driver and prior owner were yelling and intimidating in every way they could to get in the house, but I was adamant, I was not moving from the front door where they now had me backed up. My contractor and the truck driver actually chest-butted a few times and an all-out fist fight might have broke loose had the police not finally arrived. It was crazy.

My support guys were still pumping adrenalin when the prior owner and the U-Haul driver were sent on their way by the cops. I was pretty worked up too! But thank goodness my people were there supporting me because the outcome was no mistake - the foreclosure was valid. Had one piece of furniture been moved into the house, my bank would have had plenty more legal costs going through another eviction process. And how perfect was my timing? If I had arrived five minutes later, everything would have been different - the squatter would have taken possession. I got a gold star from the bank for my courage that day and many, many more of their REO listings!

The Bite Of A Pit Bull

After thirty-five years of selling real estate, I have developed a pit bull attitude. Among my other well-known and admirable traits, I can be stubborn as a mule, strong as a bear, tough as nails and obstinate as any of the best of them! But my broker only called me a pitbull when it came to For Sale By Owners because I never let go!

Three years ago I had noticed a For Sale By Owner on Federal Highway in Pompano Beach, Florida. After calling the owner for over a year, he finally listed his building at the height of the market for $1.2 Million. Unfortunately, not with me. I showed the building anyway but never came up with an offer for him. As a matter of fact, the property still had not sold after another year, so he went back to marketing it on his own again.

For yet another year that owner was persistent on his own but so was I. Christmas cards, seasonal notes, handwritten greetings and monthly newsletters made no headway in getting me in the door with him. All told, I chased that listing for nearly three years when the most glorious thing happened.

I received a phone call from a Coldwell Banker agent working in their residential division. He told me he was getting his client into a new home and the client had a building on Federal Highway that needed to be sold. The agent sent his 20% referral agreement to me and what do you know, it was the same For Sale

By Owner building I had been chasing for those three long years. I finally clinched my teeth on it!

The happy ending is that we lowered the price, set attractive terms on the property and got it sold. When I presented the offer to the seller, he said "We should have listed with you years ago!"

In the words of Winston Churchill, "Never Never Never give up!"

Like Father, Like Son

Several years ago I listed a lovely split level home on a quiet cul de sac. The owners were an older gentleman and his wife who were the most pleasant and gracious clients an agent could ever wish for. As they showed me around their pride of ownership home, there was a comfortable, warm and welcoming feel to the place.

On the lower level, the wife pointed to a closed door telling me that it was the fourth bedroom; however, it was off limits and was not be shown. She added, "When you show the house, just explain to prospects or any agents that it is a nice big bedroom with sliders to the outside, and we will make it available for them to view once we get to the walk thru stage of the sale, okay?" Not wanting to be intrusive by asking why, I simply shook my head affirmatively to confirm her request for privacy. I could work around that issue while marketing the home.

It did get me to thinking though about that fourth bedroom. Driving back to the office that day, I wondered what could be in there? Maybe they had valuables or personal belongings that were not boxed up yet. Maybe the room was used for some hobby. They were such a nice couple, I just couldn't imagine there could be anything sinister hidden behind that door.

The house was on the market for several months and then finally went under contract to close. About a week before the closing I stopped at the house to drop off some empty boxes to help with the clients' packing. While I was there the wife asked me if I would like to finally meet their only son. "Of course," I said.

I followed her downstairs to the bedroom, that private fourth bedroom, and she opened the door for me to meet Murray. Murray was about fifteen years old and, believe it or not, wearing a diaper. Imagine that? But the diaper part was not the oddest thing about him; Murray was a chimp. Yes, a real chimpanzee that my clients had raised from a baby, and this was their only son.

Murray followed the wife and me upstairs to the living room where her husband was watching television. Murray took a seat on his favorite lazy boy chair and proceeded to watch the TV like a real person. He seemed happy; what a nice boy. What I noticed most about his appearance, other than the diaper, was that he was greying and his face actually resembled her husband's face - except Murray had way more hair. When the husband would take a drink of his beer, Murray would take a drink of his milk. Murray mimicked his every move.

The house closed without a hitch, and I must say that out of the many families and kids I have met over the years in my real estate work, Murray was probably the best behaved.

Cable Guy

My brother-in-law and I worked as partners in real estate and we had a listing appointment one evening with his friends. After we finished listing their home, they recommended we go across the street because their neighbors wanted to put their home on the market too. The wife pointed to a house with the lights on and told us the couple had a new baby boy and a big friendly black Lab. She was confident they were very serious about selling. As a matter of fact, she had already promised them she'd send us over, and they would be expecting us.

We walked over and knocked on the door. When the lady answered I said, "Your neighbors said you wanted to talk to us," and we were warmly invited to come right in. As a matter of fact, she was very excited to see us and her husband added, "We've been waiting for you all day."

With a little small talk and apologies for coming by so late, the couple seemed completely happy just because we were there, offering us coffee, tea or a glass of wine. We declined the beverages and asked if we could take a quick look around the house since it was getting past 9 p.m. by then. I offered congratulations on their new little baby boy, and the woman blushed with motherly pride. She corrected me though to say her baby was a little girl. I guess my brother-in-law's friend was mistaken to say the baby was a boy.

We continued touring the house with them and asked questions about this and that. I wanted to know if the refrigerator had an ice maker, if the stove was self-cleaning and how old the water heater was. When we went into the family room there were two beagle puppies. At that point my partner nudged me sharply in the side and whispered, "Are we in the right house?" I pretty much ignored what seemed like an off-the-wall question.

As we headed back to the front room I asked the owners when they were planning to move, but the question seemed to disturb them. They frowned at me. Then the wife answered, "We're not." There was an awkward silence before the husband questioned, "Who are you? Aren't you the cable people?" In a split second, he looked at my business card he still held in his hand, then burst out laughing! Turns out they had been waiting since noon that day for the cable guy - no wonder they invited us in so quickly!

With all good cheer, we left and went next door to the couple who did have a baby boy and a big black Lab. We made certain to identify ourselves before going in!

The Don Knotts Of Real Estate

It was back in the mid-1970s and the building boom was on. I had been battling fierce Realtor competition to schmooze up to some of the local spec home builders. I will be honest, my social connections were not all that great and the world I lived in paled by comparison to the professional agents around. But word on the streets was that commissions were to be made in new home sales. I was barely paying my rent so I was a motivated guy to get out there and fight to get my piece of the pie and survive in the business.

With little self-confidence, I fumbled through cold calls again and again trying to land an appointment with a builder. By chance, I finally dogged one down who answered his phone and much to my surprise invited me to meet him at his job site. Lacking as much in common sense as I did having decent transportation, I needed him to give me turn-by-turn directions on how to get from my office in Lansdale to the site in Upper Hanover Township. I feared the appointment was probably nothing more than a patronizing accommodation from him for my weak and pathetic sales presentation on the phone, but remember I was a hungry agent being driven by the threat of eviction soon.

When I drove my Toyota Celica into the neighborhood, I discovered there was not just one house for sale, but over twenty. Visions of vast fortunes flashed before my eyes. I found my way to the spec house and prepared myself for my big moment. I leaned toward my rearview mirror and examined both my teeth and eye corners for any foreign matter, touched up my hair and straightened my tie. Feeling more dapper now, I gathered my official Realtor clipboard and placed my business card on top so I would remember to give it to him. With that, I stepped out of my car and closed the door behind ready to stride all business-like to meet MY BUILDER.

Aauughhh! I suddenly felt myself yanked backwards. I had closed the end of my tie in the car door and found myself hanging like a goose! Fumbling like a flopping bird, suspended against the side of my car, I finally got my feet under me and was able to save myself from the tightening noose around my neck.

In moments like that a man must make snap decisions on how to save masculine dignity in the face of possible public humiliation. I have found there are two options: retreat and run for your life or try to pretend it never happened. What would Barney Fife do? I chose the latter and pulled myself together to go for the appointment.

The builder and his brother were hammering away on the roof. Burly construction guys were busying about and really distracting when I finally got to have my meeting with the "boss." Unfortunately, I did not get the listing. I did, however, succeed about six months later and the builder and I became good friends, enjoying a long and successful relationship. I learned a lot during that stint with him.

Later at a party to celebrate some sales, I heard him telling a guest, so I could hear, about the day he and I first met. Apparently the brothers on the roof had seen my duffus blunder when my tie got caught. His comment to his brother was, "Here comes the Don Knotts of real estate!"

Little People

This is the story of my very first listing when I was newly licensed. As you can imagine, I was excited to show off my first professional accomplishment during our office caravan. My two-story cottage seemed to impress everyone as they toured the first floor and carefully critiqued the property. They commented on its wonderful quaint appeal and excellent location. I was beaming with a rookie's pride, until showing them the upstairs. Suddenly their eagle-eye reporting began sounding more like the emergency broadcast system alerting me to impending disaster. What did I know? I was a new agent.

The problem was the ceiling height of the upstairs bedrooms and bath. Trying to defend my listing, I reasoned that at my height, five feet even, the six and a half foot ceilings were no problem. But it was a useless debate with them. My listing had a big knock against it and to normal size adults, it was a negative that detracted from the home. From that day on, my dear fellow agents began calling me the arguing "shrimp."

My sellers were little people. They had added the second story to the cottage years ago and, for them, everything was perfect. I became determined to prove to my fellow agents that I could turn what they saw as a lemon into lemonade, and I set off to find ways to market the cottage to little people! I searched the internet for any clubs, groups or organizations that served the special needs of little people. I networked and cold called until I finally found the perfect buyers only two weeks later.

The agents in my office were amazed with my successful effort and I felt like I was the tallest person in the office the day my cottage deal closed. Beyond that, my broker used my story over and over to train and motivate other new agents on how to stand tall no matter what their real estate challenges.

The Naked Bushwhacker

We all know the showing instructions that say "Call first, use lockbox." This is a standard protocol in my area, so my assistant made the call for me and I headed off with my client to see the property. When we arrived I rang the door bell, knocked and no one answered. Then using the key to enter, I called out, "Hello? Realtor." With no reply from anyone, I led my client into the front room to begin looking around.

We had not taken more than six steps when through the kitchen door came the biggest woman I have ever seen! This woman had to have weighed 300 pounds, or more, and was naked as a jaybird. I repeat, she was huge and she was naked, but for a little pair of panties that were half buried under folds of blubber. With both arms flapping and shooing us away, her cacophony of hoots and wails came at us like the surprise attack of a wet hen! She was all over us and it was shocking.

"Get out! Get out!" she demanded. We evaporated from the place quicker than a blink and never looked back.

Landing in my car, we burst into hysterics. We were in pain from laughing so hard! Crying and laughing at the same time, we couldn't stop the mental flashbacks of our dispelling experience for nearly half an hour as I drove back to my office. It was exhausting.

To this day, I still wonder if that woman was just waiting to run out and scare us? It sure seemed like a bushwhacking and if so, I guess she had a walloping good laugh too!

The Psychologist Needs A Psychiatrist

I was asked to do a CMA for a wealthy doctor. She had her PhD in psychiatry and was a well respected psychologist in private practice. As with many medical professionals, she was a workaholic. The demands of her career were relentless. She never had children during her marriage and explained her husband of twenty-two years recently left her for lack of companionship and attention to a home life. She discovered he had been having an affair.

Upon meeting with the distraught doctor, it was obvious the strains of her divorce had taken a toll. She was anxious, however, to sell the home and buy something closer to her office where she could start a new life hoping to leave heartbreak to history. So, after listening to her drama over an hour, with great empathy I might add, I finally interrupted to say it was necessary for me to look the house over and be on my way. I left her with a box of tissues sitting there.

Gorgeous home! It was the kind with loads of dark wood trim and exquisitely fine paneling. The trappings were rich and heavy. I knew if I listed the place, simply opening the thick draperies to let in some light would transform its dark, dismal feeling immediately. There was one more room for me to see, but I had to ask the lady to unlock it for me. She did and with no forewarning, I discovered why it was locked.

There were chairs laying around sideways all over the floor and next to the wall was a huge, glass aquarium. The odor in the room was musty and terrible. It was then that she explained; her former husband had purchased a python as a pet for her. It had become her beloved "family pet," but over the years it had grown to over ten feet long. She pointed out a small cage in the corner, still stocked with rats used for snake food. The chairs served as a jungle gym for the reptile, and there on the floor was one of its shedded ten foot long skins which created a ghostly memory of the long-gone pet. The whole sight was beginning to depress me, such a disgusting thing in this beautiful house.

But wanting to show compassion for the doctor over her robbed, abandoned and rejected circumstances, I consoled her to gently say, "Well, maybe you can get a new snake."

With that she said, "Oh, I wouldn't do that. Teddy would eat it. Just look at him there behind you how big he is now." I FREAKED OUT!

The Cabbage Patch Family

Those of you who read my posts know I am an optimist; I have forward thinking. I will do whatever it takes to keep the flow flowing toward a positive end no matter what the distraction or obstacle along the way. You could say I am goal-oriented.

I recently had some buyers who I qualified as "A" buyers. They had excellent credit, good jobs, money in the bank and appeared to be all around nice people. I showed them a few properties and found one that they loved. They were ready to make an offer and asked me to come to their house to prepare the paperwork. "Of course," I said and agreed to meet there in an hour.

Arriving at their residence, they graciously invited me in and seated me, of all places, on the floor in their front room to write up the contract. I have had people ask me to remove my shoes before entering their homes, but never been offered seating on the floor when there was a fully furnished living room available. Oddly, however, placed on the sofas and chairs were Cabbage Patch dolls, ten of them in all sitting side-by-side. The clients explained they, the dolls, needed to be fed their dinner and would I mind feeding three of them? Lightheartedly, I pretended to spoon feed three of the "girls" while the wife and husband pretend-fed the other seven.

I tried to go along with this silly thing while working on the contract at the same time. I was beginning to feel a knot developing in my gut. Just about then, the wife picked one of the dolls up and explained that "Molly" had bellyache now because I had not taken the time to burp her properly. "Oh, please," I thought to myself, "I raised three children so I certainly know how to feed and burp little ones." I was actually feeling offended with her low regard for my mothering skills.

It was clear feeding time was over when the husband and wife roused to their feet and scooped up eight of the dolls, asking me to help with the other two. The husband politely said, "We will have to finish the contract in just bit if you don't mind." How could I say no to that?

Checking his watch, the husband chirped, "Yes, bath time and then to beddy-bye!"

Up the stairs the three of us went, babies in tow, to the "kids" bedroom. To my amazement, there in the bedroom were ten cribs, ten strollers and ten car seats. I "kid" you not! We then bathed them and put them to bed before quietly going downstairs to finish the contract. Two hours had passed since I arrived at their home and the offer to purchase was finally done, everything signed. What in the heck was I caught up in here? My head was spinning as I left that day.

I presented their offer and got the contract accepted on their new home. Thank heavens I found them a three bedroom home: one bedroom for the parents, one for the boy dolls and one for the girl dolls. Thank heavens I minored in psychology and sociology because otherwise I would have seriously wondered about my own sanity. Thank heavens for my title company gal, Susan, who assured me after the closing that I was completely sane, not hallucinating and not having a psychotic episode.

When it was time to close the deal, Susan had to meet my clients in the parking lot for final signatures. In their van were all ten of the Cabbage Patch dolls safely strapped in their car seats sleeping quietly. True story.

Frankly, My Dear

I've been in real estate since 1991 and have had many experiences over the years. Just the other day I had a "first." It happened during a closing.

For about a month, I had been working with an attractive lady buyer who wanted to purchase a home. She told me that after twenty-three years of marriage, her husband wanted out and was now filing for divorce. The family home had already been sold and she was renting an apartment in the meantime. She confided that she was a little nervous about starting her new life independently. And although she was close to her two children, she realized they had their own lives to lead and it was up to her now to make a new life for herself. She portrayed herself as a courageous woman trying to make the best of her changing world.

I found her to be articulate and methodical, but at times had a sense she was flying under the radar - not being completely honest with me. However, from my standpoint as her Realtor, she was an easy client to work with. Once her offer was written, the transaction went like clockwork - until the day of her closing.

Everyone was seated at the closing table. Her soon-to-be ex-husband was there to sign off any rights to her purchase, and he did so willingly. Then she began signing her paperwork for the attorney. She had literally just finished signing her last document when she suddenly lurched forward, grasping her chest. She then threw her head back and wailed. It looked like a serious emergency. Immediately we got her down on the floor and I dialed 911. It was the most dramatic scene I have ever witnessed, and especially shocking to me since I had only known her to be calm and collected at all times.

When the paramedics arrived, she was still carrying on. Oddly, they found all of her vitals to be completely normal. It was a medical mystery with a miraculous recovery, but it had certainly given everyone in the room watching a scare - except for her husband who remained unmoved by the whole event. The paramedics suggested my client follow up with her own private physician later, and they left. The closing was finished and the seller gave my client the keys to her new home. The husband walked out without saying a word.

This may be a terrible thing to say, but something makes me think my client was putting on an act that afternoon. The stage was certainly set and she did have an audience! It was like the closing scene from "Gone With The Wind," only difference was her man didn't actually come out and say those famous words, "Frankly, my dear, I don't give a damn."

You Picked A Fine Time To Panic Lucille

Call me hardhearted. Maybe I have become callous to all of humanity after so many years in real estate sales. Sometimes you reach your breaking point though, ignoring everyone else's sad story and selfishly say, "What about me?" This is what I have come to after spending one hundred twenty-three days and four hours putting together a triple-ended deal. This deal drained my gas tank fifty times and ran up so many over-the-limit minutes on my cell phone I have been forced to up my monthly plan. The pains and strains I suffered could be compared to four months' torture in a Chinese concentration camp. Well, maybe that is little exaggerated but you get my point.

My triple-ended deal was founded on a listing I had in Sylmar, California. I was representing the buyer of the Sylmar house, the seller of the Sylmar house and the same seller in buying their new house. The three legs of the transaction were contingent on each of the other legs closing. I showed the buyer of the Sylmar house twenty-two properties until he finally committed to my Sylmar listing. We negotiated the deal with me as dual agent, contingent upon the seller finding suitable housing. My sellers took two months to view every conceivable, possible, could-maybe-be-the-one until at last they made an offer that was accepted. The buyer of the Sylmar house signed their loan docs and my triple-ended deal was within three days of closing. My Sylmar sellers were scheduled to sign their loan papers at 3 p.m. on that Tuesday, with the concurrent closings to happen Friday, but when the escrow officer called me at 3:30 that day to say the clients had not arrived I began to worry.

It was not until late that night when my client's wife responded to the many voicemails I had left. Turns out her husband had a panic attack on the way to the escrow office. He ended up in the hospital that night. She said, "Just make everything go away. We can't sell the house or buy the house. It's just a bad time for our family."

So, here is the "What about me?" part. My first thought was: months of MY work down the drain and over $60,000 in commissions gone because a MAN had a panic attack? Second thought: how am I supposed to cancel my seller's purchase without giving up their deposit? Third: with loan docs in escrow, loan approved, what seller in their right mind will let them walk away unscathed? Fourth: how am I going to get my buyers' on Sylmar to give up the property they are planning to move into in three days? Inspections completed, appraisals paid for and families already packed to move twisted my already tortured mind.

Well, the gentle winds from those oceanfront properties blew in our direction. There were no lawsuits filed and everyone walked away from the deals. But me? I felt robbed. My duty was to undo the whole thing to the best of my ability, and I did, resenting every minute of it! But you know, as I enjoy a bit of sweet revenge in the telling, here is what happened later. The seller of the Sylmar house, you know the guy that had the panic attack, ended up refinancing his property, pulling cash out and investing in a foreign deal of some sort. That deal went south and he ended up losing his house in foreclosure. The poor GUY had a panic attack over moving from one house to another, but did not break a sweat putting his home on the line for a foreign investment.

Call me hardhearted, and I am not sure whether to laugh or cry. He sure picked a fine time to panic!

The Gutsy Buyer

As a full time, full service local Realtor I have loads of experience under my belt from fifteen years in the business. Despite living in a relatively small community of some 60,000 residents, we are not populated entirely with mild mannered Andy of Mayberry folks. I just happened to be the agent to represent one of them. He was a very bold and gutsy buyer who had mastered the art of getting what he wanted one way or the other. He was a take-no-prisoners type of guy and I knew from the get-go that I did not want to fall out of grace with him. I was quick to say, "Yes, sir!" and ask no questions.

He explained to me that he wanted to buy this one particular brand new home in a gated development adjacent to a popular golf course. The homes in this private community were not listed in the local multiple listing service and a co-op relationship with outside agents was not being offered. My buyer did not want to work with the builder directly nor did he want to deal with their in-house Realtor and insisted on me writing up his offer anyway. "Yes, sir!" I had no other choice but to follow his instructions.

Obediently and without question or comment, I wrote the offer, including a seller-paid commission to my brokerage on closing. Once presented, I was quite surprised that the builder agreed to the deal and accepted all the terms of our offer. Since the deal was to be an "as is" sale, the buyer and I made a thorough inspection of the property the day his offer was accepted. He understood that his purchase did not allow for any buyer contingencies, absolutely none. The closing was set for 30 days and because there was nothing else to be done in the meantime, I told my buyer I would meet him at the property to give him the keys to his new home at that time.

Thirty days came and went with a couple of courtesy calls on my part to the buyer during that time. He was not a chatty sort of guy by any means and kept our few conversations short and to the point. But finally, the closing day arrived and I arranged to pick up the keys from the builder's office and prepare a nice closing gift for my buyer. I was actually feeling really quite tickled with myself driving over there that day for having such an easy transaction.

The golf course development was very lovely, comprised of spacious lots with expensive homes in various stages of construction. It was certainly a pride of ownership place. I wondered if my client would be pleased with the ease of his purchase that was all so skillfully handled by me, his professional and highly experienced agent.

I parked in the driveway and just then my smiling buyer arrived. We greeted each other warmly and I proceeded with him into the home. I wanted to make my housewarming gift an attention-getting moment. I considered it clever and fun to include toilet paper and cleaning supplies in the welcome package together with a bottle of Dom Perignon for an official toast.

Quite to my surprise, however, my buyer stopped me short in my gift presentation and said to follow him to the backyard. I was dumbfounded! The completely dirt, un-landscaped back yard of less than four weeks ago was now fully landscaped and furnished with a gorgeous swimming pool. I have no idea how my bold and gutsy buyer got a general contractor to put in a swimming pool prior to owning the property? I have no idea how he pulled that much construction off with no one, including me, knowing that was happening. But there it was and he was now officially the new owner.

In California it is NEVER your home until the escrow closes. What if an earthquake hit before the close of escrow? Oh my goodness, my buyer invested over $100,000 in that backyard without the owner, builder or Realtors' knowledge and got away with it – but, no damage done! We did crack open the bottle of champagne and I just kept shaking my head in disbelief.

Nookie In The Pool

I am a real estate agent in Florida. Quite a few years back I had something happen that has remained etched in my memory all these years.

I was showing property to two clients. I knew them fairly well as they had purchased another property from me and were now looking to buy again. They had found a house that interested them and asked if I could set up a showing for that Sunday afternoon. When I called the listing agent he told me the owners were out of town but some friends of their family were staying at the home. There would be no problem showing it on Sunday and he assured me he would call them to let them know we would be coming by. He instructed me to pick up the house key at his office and just knock on the door when I got there; if no one was there, it would be fine to let myself in.

We drove to the house in separate cars and pulled into the driveway to park. My clients followed me to the front door. After knocking several times, no one answered so I inserted the key to unlock the door but found it was already unlocked. I opened the door and stepped into the entryway, calling out to make sure whether anyone was in the house. With no response, I was comfortable no one was there so we went in. I directed my clients to look around the front and dining areas while I proceeded toward the back of the house.

As I went around the corner into the kitchen, facing the backyard, I noticed the pool water was being churned up. It took me a second to focus in and then I saw them, a guy and a gal. The guy was sitting on the edge of the pool naked with his head leaned back and a broad old smile across his face. The gal was waist-high in water and also naked, just messing around aggressively as can be. My freak-out alarm went off inside of me and instincts kicked in to get the hell out of that place. I was experiencing an adrenalin rush for sure.

Turning around, I intercepted my clients just as they were coming into the kitchen. "We've got to go," I burst out loud. They knew right away something was up and I was trying to hide something. They sidestepped my intended block. With desperation I pleaded, "No, no, no. We've got to go." But their curiosity was a driving force and they saw it all! They were like two kids in a candy store staring out that window until I literally had to grab ahold of them and pull them toward the front door. If they had really been a couple of kids and I their mom, believe me it would have been an ear-dragging to the front door.

Now would you think an emergency room doctor, someone who sees heaven knows what each day in his occupation, could get caught up with fascination over a sight like that? His wife was just as much spellbound by this live broadcast of unbridled passion. They were sure enjoying the show!

Finally pulling them out the front door, I left no business card as evidence of having been there. I wanted it never to be known that I had escorted my clients as eye witnesses to a crime of pool passion such as this.

Recently I ran into the agent who had the home listed back them. I had been remiss to tell the agent about the incident because I knew him to be an ex-priest, but now I was ready. I told him the story and he sure got a good laugh about it. Since then I broke silence and told others too who have laughed about it. Then just a week ago, I ran into those clients and the husband asked me, "Do you remember when we went to that house?" I replied, "Yeah, I remember, Byron, I remember."

Clean Showing

It happened about eight years ago when I was still fairly new in the industry. I scheduled with the listing company to show a nice two bedroom condo on the west side of town. Having seen this unit previously while on broker caravan, I knew it to be partially updated and hoped it might be the perfect fit for my little buyers.

I received a phone call back from the company confirming the appointment and the private access code to the lock box at the unit. Arriving there, I retrieved the keys and unlocked the front door without knocking. I led my buyers in and began showing them about.

Kitchen and living room were tidy, but not in any way exceptional. Down the hallway we went. Without thinking twice, I open the bathroom door to display what I knew to be the beautifully remodeled bathroom and horror of all horrors! The sellers were in the clear glass shower stall wrapped in the heat of a passionate embrace. Oh, yes, the kind of embrace that a close-up porn film would tout!

We made a swift exit as I hollered an apology, "I'm so sorry. I had a confirmed appointment. So sorry!"

They yelled back, "No one confirmed with us!"

Since that time, no matter what anyone confirms to me, I KNOCK LOUDLY before unlocking any doors and call out LOUDLY until I am certain no one is home.

A Little Misguided Faith Perhaps?

Several years ago I was having a bad spring season in real estate when I received a cold call from a cash buyer. He was inquiring about one of my listings that was priced at $130,000. After further discussion, it turned out my listing was not going to be large enough for his family. I clarified his requirements for a home and proceeded to work with him and his wife looking at other properties. I told them I would probably need proof of funds since they were cash buyers; he assured me there was no problem.

In short time, we found the house they wanted to purchase. The asking price was $125,000 and our $120,000 offer was accepted. The owners were selling most of their furniture and my clients agreed to purchase some of it, making the physical move for both parties easier. The closing was set and we met at the bank.

It was an unusually large number of people at the closing. My buyers had their attorney with them and their minister. My broker, the listing agent, her broker, the title company rep, the sellers and the closing officer took all the available chairs so I propped myself against the wall. There was the usual stir of closing papers being passed around the conference room table. After final review, the attorney for my buyers authorized each paper to be signed, then said, "Now all we need, Richard, is your check for $120,000 and we will be done."

Richard, my cash buyer, looked around the table, took a deep breath and began to explain that this was going to be handled a little differently. "You see, I asked God for the money, and he has not given it to me yet." Then looking at his minister asked, "Have you heard anything yet?" The minister shook his head no. You could have heard a pin drop in that room! Richard's attorney began frantically combing through the ten page Purchase Contract.

The seller, who was really staying cool, asked, "When do you expect the money? Next month, next week or should we sit here and…"

Richard's attorney barged in, halting any further incriminating dribble from his client, "You have thirty days after today to complete the sale, sir."

"Okay, that's plenty of time," was Richard's response, and the room emptied with no one uttering a word.

Three weeks later the sellers received another offer and I called my buyers to say we would need a release of their contract. Richard stood his ground, insisting that he still had eight days left for the money to come.

Well, I never got a release and my buyers lost their $1,000 earnest money deposit. I guess they were holding onto a little misguided faith.

If It's Not Meant To Be, So Be It

One of my clients wanted to sell their home and buy a new one. I put their home on the market and they found the home that they wanted to purchase. Within a short time, we had both properties under contract.

During the inspection of their home, my sellers followed the inspector through the house. I followed along too. They were quiet as they observed his testing of electrical outlets and appliances. Seemed they were curious when he shined his flashlight under cabinets and behind the water heater. He continued making check marks on his clipboard as each item got a passing grade.

Down to the basement for the last part of the inspection we went. All had gone so nicely until the inspector announced a problem. He found termites. Pointing his flashlight at his discovery, my clients came out of their skin and seemed to have suddenly lost their wits.

The wife shouted out, "You devil! You're trying to ruin the sale of our house!" Both she and her husband stomped up the stairs. All the while her husband, hands raised above his head, commanded over and over, "Be gone, satan. I cast you out! Be gone!"

It took some time, but the inspector and I were finally able to calm them down. I explained that a pest control company could come and persuaded them to allow me to schedule the appointment. When the termite company arrived, they confirmed the problem and the remedy was of minor consequence.

Now that the two transactions were back on course, my clients were ready to proceed with their lender to complete the loan package for underwriting approval. Problem was they had not yet provided copies of their tax returns for the past two years, so as a courtesy I decided to go see them personally to help this final detail along.

After some pleasantries, I urged them to respond to the lender's request for this necessary paperwork. It was at this point that the husband looked directly at me and said with complete sincerity, "We have not paid taxes for the past five years."

Dumbfounded, I asked, "Why not?"

He said, "Jehovah told us we do not have to pay taxes."

No tax returns, no loan and the result was that both deals fell apart. So be it.

Sentimental Seller

I listed the home of an elderly couple who were planning to move to Arizona where their son lived. They had lived in this home for most of their fifty-six year marriage and it was clear from the beginning that the husband was having a difficult time letting the home place go. The property went under contract within a few weeks. Since they had already rented an apartment in Tucson, most of their furniture and furnishings had already been moved to Arizona by the time the escrow was ready to close.

On the day before closing, the buyers and their agent came to the property for their final walk thru inspection. The husband hovered over the proceedings like a hawk. He monopolized the conversations reminiscing his fifty-six year family history in the home. If walls could talk, even they could not have remembered intimate details of the family history like Mr. Seller did; he was definitely a sentimental old bird. Further, he was concerned that the new buyers might need his help in learning how to make everything in the house work properly. The final eye-rolling moment came when he explained for fifteen minutes how the light switch in the garage was sensitive. He demonstrated three times to the buyers and their agent how using one finger, pressed just so would make it work perfectly.

Bursting with exasperation over the old man's waylaying, the kind buyer wife said, "Maybe you should stay on a few more days to help us get used to the house?"

"Really? Oh, that would be great. I'll just leave my cot in the living room," and that was that.

When the transaction closed next day, the seller wife and her son drove away with the last of their belongings leaving the husband behind with his cot in the living room and his 1960 Fairlane in the drive. The new buyers began moving in but were somewhat surprised to find the old man there when their moving van pulled up later that day. They felt bad because he was elderly and since they offered - never believing of course that he would take them up on it - figured he would leave for Arizona the next day.

Two days later I started getting phone calls from the buyers' agent about what was now turning into an unwanted squatter situation. I phoned the seller's wife in Arizona. She insisted her husband kept telling her the family was happy he was there and that they offered for him to stay as long as he liked. I tried to explain that he needed to leave, but my words fell on deaf ears. I surmised that neither the wife nor her son wanted the old guy in Arizona.

The buyers' agent called me again. This was turning into a nightmare. I phoned the old guy's son repeatedly in Arizona, but no return call. The buyers' agent was now threatening to call the sheriff to have the sentimental seller removed, but instead it was decided to set his belongings out on the sidewalk next afternoon while he was off on an errand. He was gone by midnight that night…never to return…we think.

Wrong Exposure

I was working with a family who was relocating from the Midwest. They were very conservative folks with strong family values. Of top priority was finding a home that provided the best advantages for their children. The parents brought the kids with them to see each home we viewed so that the entire family could participate in the home buying decision.

When scheduling a property for them, I would call ahead to be certain the owners knew we were coming and let them know I would be bringing an entire family for the appointment. For one particular home, the owner explained that their grandfather who lived with them would be at the house alone when we arrived. She asked that we be considerate of the fact he was hard of hearing, and I forewarned my customers.

When we got to the house, I knocked, rang the bell and pounded on the door, but there was still no answer. My buyer family waited patiently on the porch behind me. Finally I decided to use the lockbox key and entered. Opening the door I loudly announced, "Realtor." And in single file, the family followed my lead into the entryway. Just as I turned to my left toward the living room, I was horrified to see Grandpa laying on the sofa sound asleep, stark naked. He never flinched.

With an immediate about-face, I blocked the view of my little troop before anyone saw Grandpa in his glory, then literally pushed them back through the front door. No one could understand why they didn't get to tour the house. I just kept saying, "Trust me, it has the wrong exposure for you."

Three's Company

It was in September of 1986 when I phoned my seller at 6683 Center Avenue. Mr. Kevorkian was eighty-six years old. I wanted to let him know I would be showing his home the next day at 11:30 a.m., but he did not answer nor did he respond when I called again in the morning. Since he had no answering machine, I drove over from my office ahead of time to give him a heads-up on the appointment.

His car was parked in front of the house as usual. It seemed strange he had not answered the phone when I called only half an hour earlier, but on to the business of getting the house opened up for the showing. I rang the bell, knocked on the door and with no acknowledgement from inside used my keysafe key to enter. I walked into the living room and there was Mr. Kevorkian laid back in his easy chair with "Three's Company" blaring on the television. I touched him on the shoulder, but he didn't respond. Mr. Kevorkian had passed away. It looked like he must have died in his sleep.

Just then the doorbell rang. It was the buyer couple, but this was no time for that kind of company. Trying to appear calm, I cracked open the door and whispered we would have to reschedule as the elderly owner was not prepared for the appointment. The couple were persistent and put up an argument, reasoning they had driven a long distance to see the house. So I finally acquiesced and agreed to give them a quick and limited look if they would wait on the porch for me to take care of a few details first. I found a sheet and tucked it around Mr. Kevorkian's body, carefully covering him from head to toe, and draped a large bedspread over both his body and the chair. I then pretty much strong-armed the unsuspecting couple through the house and hustled them out the door in less than five minutes. "Bye-bye and thanks for coming." Door shut!

It took only a few minutes for the paramedics to arrive after my call to them. They loaded Mr. Kevorkian on a gurney and took him to the morgue. The folks at my office later applauded me for my impressive demeanor in handling the situation; they thought I performed like a seasoned pro under the circumstances. The property did sell shortly thereafter with all the proceeds going to his church as directed under his Last Will and Testament.

I must add, this was my first year in the business specializing in expired listings.

Riding The Real Estate Coaster

I was a green agent at the reception desk one Saturday morning following New Year's Day in 2004. A young man walked in and asked for a real estate agent. Wow! I had my first client.

The young man handed me a key, and told me he needed to rent his house. He explained he had already moved and was now relocated out of state, so I wrote down all of his contact information for our property manager. Hmm? That was a quick emotional roller coaster ride for me - thought I had a client, then I didn't! Just as well it was over that quick because I'm not a fan of roller coasters anyway.

Next day the property manager invited me along to view the property with him. After we toured the place, he told me I would have to call the young man to tell him the property would not make a good rental due to its location. Wow! Maybe I'm back in for the ride again and the guy will want to list the house with me. And within a few days, I had my very first listing. Better yet, an offer came in a week later. Woohoo! I was lov'in real estate!

But, the offer was the beginning of another coaster ride. The seller's net on the offer left him bringing money to the table. I suggested he counter the offer to net zero if he just wanted to get rid of his mortgage obligation, but he insisted on accepting the offer as written with no counter.

Thirty days went by and the scheduled closing approached. The arrangements were to overnight the seller's closing package to him so he wouldn't have to make a trip back again. On the day of closing, the buyers began moving in after signing all their papers, but the seller's package never arrived at the closing office with the required check for the shortage. I had been calling my client repeatedly for twenty-four hours, but no answer. Then even worse, late in the day my client's phone indicated it was no longer in service. My coaster was peaking and I was looking down a big hill in fear for what looked like an impending catastrophe! What a terrible way to start my real estate career.

With help from my office mentor, we tracked down the seller's mother and what she explained sent me flying the rest of the way down that coaster track. My stomach turned flip-flops ten times! She said my seller was in Las Vegas; he had gone there to win the money he needed to close the deal.

Then up my coaster goes again when lucky for me, he was a lucky man. He won in Vegas and sent the money to close the deal. My first deal was done. I decided if I could survive that roller coaster ride, I could handle anything that a career in real estate would bring me!

The Perfect Storm

This is a sad story that yet today hurts to recall for two reasons. First reason had to do with love lost, second about money. The woman who was My Love at the time ended our relationship furiously. We broke up and parted on bad terms. The money reason involved a huge real estate commission I didn't get.

I had been dating this very successful gal for about a year. She was one of the hottest Realtors in our exclusive real estate area. She was making millions. We met while working at the same real estate office, and although I was a rookie agent new on the scene, it didn't take me a second to notice that every guy in that office viewed her as a goddess. She would walk into the office wearing the tightest of tops, the shortest of skirts and the tallest of shoes. She was electrifying in the mind of a guy.

During our courtship, I listed a magnificent oceanfront home. It was over six thousand square feet of living space with a living room that featured floor to ceiling windows eighteen feet high. You felt as if you were looking out from a ship on the ocean. The master bedroom was just as spectacular with panoramic ocean views that drew the beach into the room. The home's design was truly unique. The listing price was $7.2 Million.

Quite proud of my new listing, I took my girlfriend to check it out and she fell in love with the place. It would have been hard for anyone not to. She decided she wanted to buy it then and there. With oceanfront property in this exclusive enclave being a rarity, it looked to be a great investment for her. Standing in this glorious setting, she announced that day she wanted me to move in with her. I could see her heart was throbbing for what she viewed as her dream home. I guess she must have thought only a fool of a guy would have refused the invitation what with all the temptation set before him - beautiful rich woman, gorgeous house and the opportunity to land a huge commission on the sale. How could I refuse? Oh, yes, the sacrifices I was willing to make for My Love. So, I put the contract together, negotiated the price and she was buying the property for $6.9 Million!

The closing was to take place ninety days from contract date. Old rule: never good to stretch out a closing because a lot can happen over three months of time to change circumstances. In my case, circumstances were changing. We had been fighting like cats and dogs and during those months I made up my mind that I could never live with that woman. She was far too aggressive, too forceful and way overdominating for me. But how do I tell her? She had put up a huge nonrefundable deposit and this was her dream home. I knew she wasn't buying the house just so she and I could live together, but it was a significant part of it.

The clock was ticking on the escrow and I knew I had to tell her. My conscience was screaming to do the right thing, but my bank account yelled, "No! Don't give up the fat commission." I deferred to my good conscience and prepared my speech. I would massage the idea that her investment decision to buy was a really smart thing and even though I was not going to move in, that wouldn't prevent her from acquiring her dream home. Boy, was I wrong.

She was furious. She not only wanted "out" of our relationship, but even more she wanted "out" of her contract to buy the home. In the fury of her storm, she went to my boss and told him I had tricked her into buying the property. When my boss called me into his office to discuss the situation, he informed me that since her large deposit was nonrefundable, she had to go through with the sale. That was not going to sit well with this angry woman who was no longer "My Love" nor my loyal client.

Then a miracle happened. I truly think it was the fury of this woman that fueled what came next. A hurricane hit our affluent community. The hurricane caused extensive damage to the dream home, still under contract to purchase. THAT powerful and furious storm was so damaging that a particular clause in the contract could now be used to get her out of the deal and her entire deposit returned. Talk about the perfect storm that came at a perfect time. It was a miracle made for me and the storm that saved my life!

So, my ex-girlfriend did not buy the house. I did not collect a commission. Moral of the story? Do not mix business with pleasure! It was a very costly experience for me.

Warm Reception

I was getting the final details finished for the Open House at my townhome that afternoon. Being a Realtor, of course I knew all the right things to do for marketing my property. I wanted everything picture perfect because making that all-important first impression on prospective buyers is vital. Double whammy with the first impressions because as the listing agent and representing myself, they would be scrutinizing me too! I am abundantly aware how buyers look things over with a critical eye, and just one little detail that looks bad can sway their interest in a negative direction. My cleaning gal did a thorough job the day before, window cleaning company as well. I even bought fresh bouquets of flowers and filled several vases for around the house. And I, too, would be handsomely groomed!

It was a clear and beautiful Sunday in autumn. Leaves were turning color, all yellow and red, and the temperature outside was refreshing though a bit nippy for a November day in Connecticut. At the last minute, I decided it would be nice to have a fire in the living room fireplace to add a warm touch on a day like this. So I collected up several good sized pieces of wood from my wood stack outside, placed them inside the fireplace and lit the wadded newspaper.

With less than an hour before show time, I dashed upstairs to hop in the shower and make myself ready. Maybe ten minutes in the bathroom and I started to smell smoke. Very quickly the smoke got heavier. I wrapped a towel around my dripping wet self and flew downstairs. The living room was filled with so much smoke I could hardly see. Yes, you guessed it, I forgot to open the flue.

I held my breath trying not to inhale as the air darkened with smoke still pouring out of the fireplace. My eyes were burning and watering badly, but groped my way across the room. It was a fumbling struggle until I finally laid my hand on the lever for the flue and flipped it open - I say "flipped" because it was really hot.

With my open house to start in twenty minutes, I became frantic to get the smoke cleared out. I threw open every window in the place and used my towel to fan the air before running upstairs to dress and try to spit-polish my appearance. Over the buzz of my electric razor, I heard the faint sound of a siren. It was growing louder by the minute and much as I dreaded it, I just knew it was heading to my house.

That quickly, my townhouse was surrounded by a squad of fire trucks. Seems a neighbor saw smoke and called 911. Luckily I got to the door just as the firemen starting knocking or most certainly they would have put their axes into making an emergency entrance. Assuring them that all was fine, no fire emergency only an accidentally closed flue, they retreated to their trucks and began dismantling their fire fighting paraphernalia to leave. And as bad timing would have it, pulling up to park were my first open house guests, two cars and then a third.

You have all heard that baking bread makes your house smell warm and inviting. Well, the smell of burning wood throughout a house gives a very special autumn scent, if you didn't know. Yes, I created a warm reception for my guests that day with my special autumn aroma.

Broker Caravan Blunder

On a bright sunny morning in beautiful Southern California, my office was taking our weekly broker caravan of new listings. On this particular day, we had five properties to view. The caravan totaled four vehicles, each filled to car pooling capacity with agents from my office. Arriving at the last property on the previewing tour, our troop descended on the property like a swarm of fussy bees. The home was in an older neighborhood with a fairly small lot. It was at the bottom price point for the community, but from the outside looked to be in pretty good shape. Each home on the street had a fenced front yard with chain link that extended to the sidewalk and a simple flip-latch gate for entering. Side by side, these homes were cookie-cutter design with minor exterior variations.

Clomping like a hot and thirsty herd of cattle onto the old front porch, our group of agents was getting a little testy from the long morning drive around the city. One of them knocked on the door but got no response. While waiting, another agent who was obviously beyond impatience over this delay began looking around for a lockbox to gain entry to the house. Not finding one and still no answer at the front door, she spouted sarcastically, "The listing agent didn't even bother to install a lock box here."

Finally giving up, everyone started to head toward the cars for our return to the office. Just then the front door slowly opened and a young gentleman peered out. He had the most quizzical look on his face. Turning back on a dime, our take-charge broker took hold of the door to quickly usher us in. In his commanding tone he barked, "We are here from (blank) Realty Associates and would like to view your property." With that declaration made, the broker walked past the still silent resident standing in the doorway. Our troop of minion agents poured in like thick goo overtaking the place.

Once inside, we worked our way through each room, commenting on size, shape and desirability. The home really was in pretty good shape, I thought. We opened closets and cupboards to evaluate utility. Someone raised the throw rug to check the condition of the hardwood floor while other agents sniffed around like search hounds looking for any flaws of note. Another agent, finding the bathroom door ajar, pushed it open to find a mother brushing a youngster's hair, ostensibly in preparation for school. The surprised woman looked up, saying nothing, and our agents passed by, eyeballing the place up and down before moving on.

All professional snooping complete, we filed out the front door where the young man was still standing. Each of us gave him a thanks as we passed by, a curt thanks that was really more like a quick, passing blow than a gracious farewell. He responded with a little smile in a tortured sort of way, and closed the door.

All loaded back into our cars and ready to leave, an astute observation befell us. The "For Sale" sign next to the chain linked fence in the front yard was actually on the opposite side of the fence. The sign was on the adjacent property! We laughed for weeks trying to imagine what those poor people must have thought when we came barging into their home that morning.

No Time To Smell The Roses

Office caravanning is an interesting activity for realtors. There are a lot of unwritten rules that go with the territory, and some of the rules can change without notice depending on circumstances. That's the problem. You might only know one changed when you violate it. And, heaven help new agents, they just have to catch on by keeping a close eye on the old pros who generally run on automatic pilot.

The most universal unwritten rule, though, is one that says, "If you want me to impress your seller by attending caravan at your listing, you had better attend mine too." I figured that one out very early in my career and have never violated it. It's a professional courtesy. Agents in my office are really good about those kind of courtesies.

For our office caravans, we generally carpool to see the new listings each week and have the routine down pretty pat. Once parked, we all walk in single file up the walkway, into the house and follow the leader through the home. There is a certain cadence that is set so no time is wasted and agents can get back to the office for their business. We keep the caravan moving continually. If the weather is miserable, Rule No. 2 is "no talking and move faster." Most of the unwritten rules are really just good common sense.

During one of our caravans recently, there was a brand new agent walking right in front of me. She stopped abruptly and leaned over to smell one of the beautiful roses growing alongside the walkway.

Big mistake for a Realtor in a line of other Realtors rushing to get through a caravan of new listings.

I didn't stop.

I knocked her right into the rose bushes.

Rule No. 3: Realtors don't have the luxury to stop and smell the roses.

Open House Stranger

At a recent open house, there was a really scruffy guy who came in to look around. He said he was in a lower price range, so I offered to email him a list of other properties. We chatted briefly and he left. Several minutes later he came back and said he had locked his keys in his car. He was wondering if he could borrow my car to run home to get his spare.

I, of course, told him I didn't really feel comfortable handing my brand new car over to a complete stranger, and asked why he couldn't walk home since he had told me earlier he lived only four blocks away. To this he replied, "I don't like to walk uphill."

With that, he picked up the pen from the counter where we were standing and scratched his name off my sign in sheet. He intentionally dropped the pen on the floor and walked out the door in a dramatic huff without a word. He slammed the door closed.

Feeling more than a little unsettled, I had my cell phone in hand, ready to make an emergency call as I looked out the front window. All I could see were my open house balloons that had been yanked loose and floating free up to the sky.

My Open House Disaster

Here is an open house story that I do not tell about too often. I must beg your indulgence to understand this happened when I was young and foolish; I am older and wiser today. It was actually my very first open house ever as a new licensee. I had just graduated from college the week before and joined my family's real estate company. Willing to jump right into my new career, the open house was on that Sunday.

The house I would be showing was a beautiful home in Fairfield, Connecticut. It had just been remodeled with new kitchen, baths and hardwood flooring throughout. In fact the floors were so new, finished with polyurethane, there was still brown construction paper down for protection until the shiny stuff was fully cured. The house was vacant with no furniture moved back in yet.

So being a recent college graduate about to join the workplace, my friends decided to take me out for a Saturday night celebration. I was feeling quite-the-guy with my degree and all, so off to a disco we went to whoop it up. For sake of contemporary reading, let me remind you that in the 1980's disco was a happening! I have some vague memory of doing shots of tequila all evening at the club. It turned into one big blur, but there is some hazy snapshot in my brain of someone offering to drive my car for me as we left the club. I was really in a stupid stupor.

Next morning I woke up in an unfamiliar place; I was confused and disoriented. I was in a bed, pretty comfortable actually, with a young lady next to me who was unclothed. My new "friend" began kissing me and giggled playfully, "Good morning, sleepyhead." Now this scared me really bad and got my attention quickly because I had never seen this girl before. Then it dawned on me that I had to be at an open house at 11 a.m. "What time is it?" She answered so sweetly, "10:30."

Panic button time! Here I am naked in a stranger's bed. I don't know who she is or where I am, and I have to be at an open house in thirty minutes. Turns out that I am about a twenty-five minute drive from the Fairfield house, so I weeded through the blankets looking for my clothes to get moving fast. "Where are my clothes? Where are my clothes?" I was becoming desperate now.

"Sweetie, you got sick on the way home last night so I put them in the washing machine for you this morning."

I came unglued and probably frightened her with my loud retort, "I have to be at an open house in twenty minutes, and I have no clothes to wear?"

With that she hopped up, leaving the room and returned with a sympathetic smile, tossing me a t-shirt and pair of gym shorts and saying, "These are the biggest clothes I own."

I had no choice, so pulled on my pathetic open house outfit. It was a pair of green gym shorts and yellow t-shirt. The shirt was so tight I could barely stretch it down over my stomach to meet the waste band of the crotch-tight shorts. I put on my dress shoes, black socks and out the door I went. Car keys in hand I fled in my ridiculous costume.

READY, WILLING & (unbeliev)ABLE

Finally parked in the driveway, I retrieved the open house signs from the garage and tried pushing the metal posts into the ground in the front yard. Either the area was once a quarry of solid granite or I had exhausted every bit of my manly strength in the morning's fiasco, but I could not get one of them to stick down in the ground. Struggling like a clumsy fool, any nosey neighbors must have been laughing to see me fall over twice trying to bear some weight on the darn posts. Now I not only looked like a moron in my outfit, but I had grass stains on my knees and elbows too. Frustrated as heck, I abandoned the effort and leaned both signs against the mailbox and went in the house.

Since there was no furniture to sit on, I just crashed in a corner of the living room floor. I was feeling wretched, dressed in this elf outfit and all, but hey, I did it to myself. I began hoping no one would show up so I could save some vestige of self-esteem by keeping this whole thing a secret. I was nauseous, thirsty and still dizzy-headed, then dozed off to sleep on the floor.

Next thing I knew, I woke up to the sound of some people talking. Glancing at my watch I realized I had been passed out for over two hours and a couple of buyers were walking in the front door. I pulled myself together and apologized for my appearance, then took them around the house pointing out the wonderful major improvements. The husband wanted to see the basement to check out the new furnace and the wife continued looking around upstairs. I followed hubby down and he was quite fascinated looking at the new oil burner. Then we made our way back up. I was feeling nauseous again. OMG! I was really holding back and trying not to throw up, and lucky for me, they were ready to leave. I gave them my card and made another quick apology for my appearance as they left.

Once the door closed behind them, I ran for the newly remodeled guest bathroom around the corner. In my urgency, the brown construction paper under my dress shoes gave way. The paper slipped and my legs flipped, and I landed flat on my back. I think I must have been knocked out for a minute before picking myself up. I groped my way along the wall getting my miserable self finally into the bathroom, still alive somehow, then stared at my pale face in the mirror for ten minutes like a zombie. I felt like something the cat dragged in!

The most positive thing ended up happening though. The same couple ended up buying the house. Out of hundreds of sales since then, I will say none have been more memorable to me as that one. I am still a little ashamed to confess the story publicly, but I promise you this, my professional behavior has improved dramatically over the years since that open house disaster.

Cue The Deer

I loved the movie <u>Funny Farm</u> starring Chevy Chase. "Cue the deer" was a phrase they used in the movie to mean it was time for a trained deer to enter the scene. The idea was to impress some buyers at a house that was for sale.

I experienced a similar scene one day when I was showing my listing to a prospect. The property was a log home built in the middle of a gorgeous forest setting on the Scioto River. The thick blanket of fresh snow, blue sky and woodsy backdrop created a picture perfect moment as we enjoyed the view out the glass wall into the backyard. There was a deer resting peacefully next to a large pine and a few squirrels scampering about. It was a scene I couldn't have choreographed had I planned it.

Then we realized something was wrong. The deer had a broken leg. Sadly touched by the sight, I insisted my buyers leave and come back later after I contacted Animal Control for help. Because it was a Saturday, they sent a police officer who arrived some thirty minutes later. He pulled up and got out of his car carrying a rifle, a really big one. I motioned him in the direction of the backyard.

Just about then, another realtor pulled up who was intending to show the property. In a big, jolly voice he cackled, "Where's Rambo going?"

I had never met this realtor before but even so, buried my head in his chest as he came walking up so I wouldn't hear the gun go off. So much for "cuing the deer" on my movie set that day!

The Open House Viewing

It was a classic Southern California day to hold open house. The sky was blue, temperature perfect. Located in a popular family neighborhood, this two-story home was well priced so I was certain my advertising would attract plenty of lookers to view the property. Little did I know the viewing was going to be turned around on me.

As it goes many times with open houses, there can be several buyer prospects visiting at the same time. The lookers come in waves it seems. This was the case at about 3 o'clock that day. I was juggling my attention between two different couples. They had finished touring the upstairs bedrooms, garage, backyard and main floor when a third couple arrived. In an effort to make my final connection with the first two, I smiled at the new arrivals who promptly made their way upstairs.

After handshakes and a gracious farewell to the two couples, I realized the third couple had not come downstairs. They were older folks, probably in their late seventies, so in consideration of their age I decided I should slow my eager salesman tempo down before going up to properly introduce myself. I collected my business card and a flier from the kitchen counter and headed up the stairway. I could now offer them my undivided attention.

As I reached the upstairs landing, it seemed suspicious that all the bedroom doors were closed. With more than an inkling of concern, I slowly opened the master bedroom door and peeked in. To my surprise there on the bed, bare-bottomed and in rapid, hip thrusting motion, was the old couple. They were having sex! The ghastly sight of all that white, jiggling skin was simply too much for me to bear so I quickly closed my eyes to block out the scene, then quietly pulled the door closed.

I think I was experiencing post-traumatic shock because I somehow found myself back downstairs standing in the kitchen. An echoing voice in my head began screaming, "Emergency! Call Stephanie!" Stephanie is my best friend and has always been a lifeline for me in times of desperation like this. Flipping open my phone, I speed-dialed. Ringing and ringing, but no answer. I was stuck. I was alone in the kitchen at my open house with this awkward and disturbing situation going on in the bedroom. Can you imagine?

Then I heard a small noise from upstairs that seemed to snap me out of my stunned condition. I could hear the faint sound of conversation and saw the couple coming down the stairway. They were chit-chatting with each other same as if they were taking a stroll in the park on a Sunday afternoon. I must have looked like a ghost standing in the kitchen. I still had the cell phone to my ear and my mouth was hanging open. They glanced my direction, smiled politely, and said, "Thanks for the viewing!" And just that quick, they were out the front door.

Taking a deep breath, I collected my thoughts and decided to close the open house early. I was still upset and shuddered at the thought of revisiting the scene of their indecent crime upstairs, but since I was responsible for turning off all the lights before leaving I had no choice. Thank goodness when I checked the master suite the bed was made and there was no leftover evidence of what had taken place there. I locked up and headed for home.

While driving down the block, the parting words of the old couple continued ringing in my ears, "Thanks for the viewing." I'd like to get the chance to tell them, "Thanks loads for the unexpected viewing I got!"

It Was Quite A View

I am an experienced Professional ABR Certified agent. I was representing a very high end builder and marketing a home in an exclusive country club community. This estate was priced at $6.5 Million with every amenity you can imagine. It was located on the waterfront with landscaping that highlighted the water view from the grand room and office like a master artist's rendering. Monet would have been impressed.

Each time I presented the property, I told a wonderful story describing each room and every feature, especially emphasizing the waterfront view. The wealthy buyer prospects appreciated my detailed information. My intent was to form an intimate and personal relationship between them and the property as we made the tour. One of the high points of the floor plan was an appealing office. It was finished to the nines with custom mahogany cabinetry, carved with fine, detailed craftsmanship. The built-in desk was perfectly positioned to take advantage of the waterway view. Behind the desk was a fixed monitor behind a dark glass that was wired for all news reports, sports and constant ticker feed of the latest stock exchange information.

On this one particular day, I was in the plush office of the estate presenting the property to a man and woman. They stood on either side of me as I pointed out the latest technologies installed in the room. With a remote control in hand, my canned delivery was to spread my hands toward the draperies and touch the button to reveal the gloriously beautiful waterfront view. Slowly and quietly, the drapes opened and in perfectly synchronized timing, a boat was passing by. I was just about to say, "Behold, our beautiful and peaceful view," when we saw that there were two naked people in the boat. Not only were they naked, but they were in doggy position. To make the shocking sight worse, the woman had the largest breasts I have ever seen.

All three of us were speechless, frozen in disbelief. Then the wife kindly said, "Well, yes, this is quite a view."

Those buyers did not buy the house.

I Killed My Seller

Several years ago my company sponsored an event that was called "The Tailgate Tour of Homes." It was to be an open house occasion for the public that included eight select homes in the area. The homes would be held open on that particular evening from five to eight o'clock. We arranged for several agents to be stationed at each of the homes and planned to serve champagne and strawberries to the guests, a classy little touch.

The homes on tour ranged in price from $60,000 to $500,000. I would be greeting guests at my listing which was the lowest priced property. It was a small house, little more than eight hundred square feet, but an absolute doll house with the best curb appeal on the block. The owners, Ron and Don, were a cute little couple. They wanted their home to be perfect for the onslaught of visitors we were expecting at this well advertised event. They asked me if there was anything they could do to make the house more appealing and I made several suggestions. One was to either replace one area of carpeting with new carpet or tile the space. Don said he would get right on it. I also recommended a bathroom remodel as well as a few additional cosmetic repairs. Don said he would get right on it. And he did! He was intense about making sure everything would be perfect for the open house.

On the evening of our tour, there were people lining up outside on the sidewalk ahead of time. I peeped out the front window and was thrilled with the turnout. I began to wonder whether the buyer interest was due to the low price, the convenient hour of the event or just snoopy neighbors wanting to look. Whatever the answer, I was delighted with what was looking like an enormous public response.

Don and Ron were ready to leave the house just before five and told me they would be hanging out at the neighbor's so they would be out of the way. They were excited with all the prospects waiting outside and nervous as heck! We agents had created a buzz of excitement.

Just then Don remembered he had forgotten one last detail, a picture he wanted hung upstairs in the newly remodeled master bathroom. He asked me if I could hold the guests downstairs only a few minutes while he ran upstairs quick, hammer in hand, to add this finishing touch. So, with Don upstairs I opened the front door and began greeting the guests.

The downstairs rooms were filling up fast as the line of people continued streaming in. I was anxious not to lose any prospects for the little house, so I skipped upstairs to tell Don to hurry with his minor task. As there were people waiting at the front door, I needed to start sending folks upstairs to make more room.

Reaching the top of the steps I barged into the master bedroom. My heart stopped. There on the floor at the foot of the bed was Don. He was not breathing. I just knew he was dead. "Oh, my God," I heard myself say aloud. "What am I to do? What am I to do? Oh, my."

Just then I heard people coming up the stairway. To avert a traumatic catastrophe in the little house now crammed full of people, I knew I had to keep the situation quiet. I quickly closed the bedroom door behind me. Standing in front of it like a sentry guard, I began apologizing to the stream of lookers passing by in the hallway, saying the owner had taken ill and unfortunately there would be no viewing of the master bedroom. A fellow agent came up the steps chatting her sales talk to some prospects and I pulled her aside, taking firm grip of her arm. I looked her in the eye and told her to stand in front of the bedroom door and under NO circumstances let anyone go in because the owner was ill.

I raced down the steps to find my senior agent and whispered that we had a major emergency upstairs. Posturing with a playful look, she asked whimsically what could possibly be wrong? We were in our glory with the success of this event. "The seller is dead upstairs!" I whispered. She started to laugh and I didn't blame her because what I said came out of left field! But when she looked directly at me, it was clear this was no joke. She clasped her face with both hands and whispered, "Oh my God. Call 911 immediately." I did.

The house was still packed when the fire and rescue trucks showed up only minutes later. They had to park in the middle of the street due to the open house traffic jam. Four paramedics pushed through the crowd and I led them upstairs explaining the situation as quietly as I could to avoid pandemonium. My senior agent then started clearing the house, ushering everyone out the door while explaining there had been a medical emergency. She handed out cards and fliers with gracious aplomb till the last guests were gone.

I am telling my story here and have told it to people at many different real estate events over the years. I tell them about the great success of our "Tailgate Tour of Homes." I not only received an offer on the house the following day, but three more within a couple of days. All four of our agents there that evening picked up plenty of new buyers to work with as well.

On one hand it was a great event, but on the other it was the most horrible open house I have ever had. I lost one of my favorite clients that evening and for a while afterward, felt guilty. Maybe if I had not suggested Don make the repairs he would still be alive? Maybe he worked too hard in getting the house ready? Maybe the stress that it had to be perfect was too much for him to take. For weeks afterward, I honestly believed that I killed my seller.

The Price Was Right

The most bizarre showing I have had in my career was at the home of Tilly Anderson. She was the sweetest little old lady I had ever met. Demur and white-haired, her passivity was even more pronounced because she was deaf as a doorknob. She would agree politely with anything a person said; you knew she never actually heard a word.

I listed her home with her caring son who, as her conservator, knew that Tilly could no longer stay in the home caring for herself. There in the house, papers signed, Tilly agreed to the arrangements being made and seemed content in accepting the changes to come. I put the house on the market.

The for sale sign was installed and the very next day I received a call from an interested buyer. I arranged to meet the lady at the property next morning at 10 a.m. Held up in traffic, I arrived ten minutes late and my buyer prospect was waiting patiently in front of the home. I introduced myself, asking her to wait until I went in and spoke with the owner. Knocking loudly on the door, I got no response from Tilly. I could hear the television blaring so I used the key to go in. Knowing she did not hear me banging on the door, I hollered a big hello her direction. She was sitting in her Lazy Boy staring at "The Price Is Right", captivated it seemed with the drama Bob Barker created.

READY, WILLING & (unbeliev)ABLE

After turning on lights and opening a few curtains, the dark little house was ready for my prospect to come in. We walked through the living room, dining area and kitchen, then passed by the den where Tilly was sitting so as not to interrupt her show. Upstairs we viewed the bedrooms and bath. Once downstairs the interested buyer asked if she could bring her mother to see the home as she lived just up the street. I told her that would be fine and I would wait for them. She yelled a "thank you" in the direction of the den and left.

When I went into the den to talk to Tilly, she was still staring at the television. Her eyes were open but she was motionless. I went closer to make sure she was okay and touched her hand. Ice cold. Tilly Anderson was dead.

I immediately called her son and told him what I had just discovered. He was leaving his office and asked me to call the police; he was on his way. It seemed like everyone arrived at the same time, the police, the paramedics and Tilly's son, and then my client pulled up with her mother.

The client asked what had happened and I explained that the elderly owner had passed away. She and her mother seemed sadly touched by this. As I was going back toward the house, the client caught up to me, followed by her mother, and said, "I know this probably isn't the right time, but would it be okay if I just showed my mom the house quickly?" I stiffened like a board. There was no way she just asked me that. I don't remember responding, but they went on in the open door. A few minutes later, they came out and approached me still standing in the front yard. The prospective buyer said, "When things settle down, please call me. I want this house." Was that a heart cold as ice?

My mind was a blur, but a couple of months later they did buy the house and the price was right.

The Sound Of Silence

This is an incident that happened to my husband back in the mid-1990's. We are both Realtors and work together as a team. Scott asked me to line up a showing at one of our office listings. He had some buyers who had already driven by the place and were anxious to see inside early the next morning. The owner's brother was living in the home, so I confirmed the appointment with the brother who said he would be at work and Scott could use the lockbox key to bring the customers in.

Scott showed up the next morning with the buyers. He was surprised to find the brother's car parked in the driveway. He went to the door and knocked, but nobody answered. He went around to a side window where he yelled the brother's name, hoping to get his attention, but no response. With the screen door locked from the inside, the key to the front door did him no good. The back screen door was also locked from the inside.

Scott was getting concerned at this point so he asked the buyers to wait in the car for him while he tried to get into the house. He poked a small hole through the front screen just enough that he could unlatch it and then unlocked the door using the key. When he went into the living room, he found the brother dead on the couch wearing nothing but a t-shirt, underwear and socks. He had died of a heart attack the evening before.

Scott called the police. Going back outside to where the buyers were still waiting, he explained that they would not be able to see inside the house. As the police and fire department arrived at the scene, the buyers made arrangements with Scott to meet again at the property the next day. They ended up purchasing the home and ………they even bought the couch………!

The Spirit Of The Deal

In 2006, I was looking for a property for myself and my fiancé. We saw a home listed as "Owner/Agent" and took a tour of the place. We not only fell in love with the home but the owner as well. She was a single lady, never married. She was successful, beautiful, friendly and sophisticated, yet very down to earth. She was wonderfully authentic, and I connected with that immediately. I made the comment to my fiancé at one point, "She's a good soul."

We put in an offer and it was accepted. On the day of our physical inspection, there was what we thought to be a gardener at the house. He gave me a creepy vibe. As my fiancé and I tailed the inspector around the house, the gardener seemed to be shadowing our every move. He was elusive. His response to my friendly smile was an evil glare. My fiancé paid it no attention even though I kept tugging his arm to take closer notice of the guy. When we left, my fiancé jokingly told me I should have just piped up to say, "What's up, Cabana Boy?" I failed to see his humor.

Two days later, I got up in the morning and turned on the news. The headline was about a gruesome crime committed on the west side of town, two people were dead. Oh, my gosh! It was our house and the owner/agent was dead. The guy we thought to be the gardener earlier was in fact her boyfriend.

The lady had no children, her parents were deceased and next of kin were two brothers, both of whom were under conservatorship authority in another state. A cousin from California stepped in to act on behalf of our deceased seller. Now I was having second thoughts about buying the house. I decided to research "stigmatized properties" and found that they were generally decreased in the value from 10%-50%. And although such a crime is not a required disclosure in our state, I interpreted that the crime did create a "material change" in the property.

Nevertheless we loved the home and decided to proceed, but requested a 10% price reduction. The cousin discussed this with the brothers, but the attorneys representing the brothers stated the property was already under market and in fact tried to renegotiate the price up! The lawyers threatened to keep our earnest money if we cancelled the contract.

In the end, we bought a "stigmatized property" for full price, at the top of the market, but have loved it nonetheless. I have always felt that if the woman's spirit was still around in the house, she was welcome.

Undaunted In North Las Vegas

I am a real estate agent in Nevada. My buyer, Anita, was a jovial woman who was as outgoing and friendly as anyone I had ever known. She was a big woman and when she greeted you with a hug, you knew she meant it. She was a people lover. Self-assured in both her size and personality, she radiated a positive and confident flare that was contagious.

We had viewed several homes and it became clear that Anita was just as concerned about who the neighbors were as what the house looked like. After each home we toured, she would seek out someone on the block to engage in conversation to find out about the people in the area.

One day I showed Anita and her husband a house in North Las Vegas. This home was one of the cutest and swankiest Vegas homes I had ever seen. When we finished looking around, Anita caught up with a neighbor who was puttering in their yard. The neighbor proceeded to tell us that eight different people on eight different occasions had committed suicide in the house directly across the street.

To my surprise, Anita was totally unaffected by this and quipped, "Then there's not much to worry about. Sounds like all the troublemakers are DEAD!"

Was It Something I Said?

Back in 1989 I was working with a couple who were interested in looking at foreclosure properties. We had viewed three homes, all located north and west of town, and arrived to see the last one on my list. This one was in a subdivision on the east side of town and I could tell my customers were most interested in it.

After we finished the tour and I was locking up, the husband asked, "How is the crime in this area?"

I replied, "It's really good."

As I walked them back to their car, I was expecting them to instruct me to write up an offer right away. Based on their comments while looking the place over, I had every reason to believe this property was the one they wanted.

Then the husband asked, "What did you mean by good crime?"

I said, "You know, attempted robbery, car jacking, that kind of stuff."

He started his car, and saying they would get back to me, abruptly drove away. Next day I left a message on the husband's cell phone, but he didn't return my call. Then, two days later I received a call from him. He was curt, stating that although he thought I was the funniest real estate agent he had ever met, they would no longer need my services and he hung up. That left me confused. Had I missed something in the communication?

As life would have it, I ran into the couple several days later in a movie line. I politely asked if they had found a house yet and the husband replied that the subdivision I showed them, the one with the good crime, was not something they were comfortable with. I explained that I had personally verified all police information for the neighborhood and knew the crime was really good, as good as any of the best neighborhoods in our city.

But with that, he grabbed his wife's arm and walked away from the line where we were standing, saying, "Then I guess we'll move to another city if you think robbery and car jacking is good!"

Was it something I said?

Oh My!

I was meeting with a nice, older couple one afternoon to look at a condo. The showing instructions were to "go, knock and use the lock box." After knocking several times and ringing the bell, no one answered. So using the lock box key, we entered the home.

We wandered around a bit, conversing back and forth as we considered the pluses and minuses of the place for them. I could tell they were somewhat interested.

Then down the hallway towards the bedrooms we went. The wife opened a closed bedroom door on our left and there stood a young man in front of a full length mirror. His back was towards us. He was dressed in women's underwear, pale pink and lacey with matching bra. The panties were wedged in a way that his butt-cheeks were fully exposed. He had a pink, fluffy boa tossed around his neck and stood about six feet tall in red, spiked heals. A white garter belt was only loosely holding up his black, fishnet nylons. He was in pleasure land with himself and so lost in his private world he never even noticed us.

"Oh, my!" the wife whispered. I couldn't help taking a double-take before quietly pulling the door closed, and we tiptoed out the front door. Needless to say, my nice, elderly clients lost all interest in the place after that bizarre scene.

Whips And Chains, Oh My!

An older couple walked into the office during my floor time one day and were interested in buying a condominium. They explained what they were looking for, laying out only two priorities; the unit had to be located on the ocean and have two bedrooms. Within their budget, this was a realistic order for me to fill. We planned to meet the next morning at my office to begin viewing some properties, and I lined up our schedule.

We started off at an oceanfront complex called the Reef. It was a nice building, reasonably priced and had direct access to the beach. We were greeted by the listing agent in the lobby. His name was Phil and as I had met him previously, I knew him to be a nice guy. He led us upstairs to show the apartment and when we walked into the main living room the ocean view was terrific. I noticed my clients looking at each other and could tell by their expressions that they were delighted with what they saw. My thoughts immediately went into high gear; this was going to be a slam dunk. I was already calculating my commission.

The master bedroom was next on the tour. All was looking so good for the sale at this point that I was nearly waltzing across the room to open the bedroom door, but my happy commission thoughts were quickly erased when we looked inside. There was no furniture in the room. No, I take that back. There was no "normal" furniture. Where the bed was supposed to be was a "sling." As I had never seen one before, I was not actually sure what goes on with one, but I knew after seeing the stockade and chains anchored to the ceiling something here was weird. On the floor were whips, paddles and other sexual paraphernalia.

My clients looked at each other again, but not with smiles. Their faces were flushed. Frowning and obviously disgusted, the wife promptly said she had seen enough. Despite Phil's effort to act as if nothing was out of the ordinary, they were no longer interested in continuing the tour. Phil, however, kept on with his sales pitch talking about how large the room was and that the ocean view from the window was spectacular. He pulled back the drapes in an effort to hold them there longer, but my clients turned away.

They made a beeline to the front door and I followed. We got into the elevator together and I found myself lost for words. Exiting into the lobby, I finally found it within myself to apologize to them. I told them I had no idea the room would be that way, but they would hear no part of it. They were insulted and said I should have known ahead of time and that Phil should have warned me. They went on to say it was appalling.

I felt spanked in the face. I tried throwing myself at the mercy of the court, nearly pleading to convince them the next condos were going to be nothing like this one, but to no avail. They replied they did not wish to see them with me. They did not want to do business with me anymore.

When Phil came down to the lobby, I was totally disgusted with him. I asked him how he could show that dungeon in good conscience without warning a fellow agent. His reply was, "If I had told you, would you have shown it?"

I said absolutely NOT! To which he replied, "There's your answer."

A Lewd Encounter

I received a cold call while at the office from a rather deep-voiced woman who said she had a cleaning service business in Boca Raton. She was interested in a one bedroom condo so we made a plan to meet and look at a few places.

We looked at two different units and then headed to the third with her following me in her car. The first two units were occupied and fully furnished, but the third one was vacant. While unlocking the door, I had a call on my cell and told my customer to go on ahead and look around the unit while I took care of some quick business. Standing in the hallway outside the front door, I answered my call.

Couple of minutes passed and I heard the customer calling my name. She was wanting me to come see the walk-in closet. I finished on the phone and went into the bedroom thinking she must have been pleased to discover the large walk-in. As I turned the corner to look into the closet, I could not believe my eyes.

My customer was standing in the closet in panties and bra making sexual poses!

Embarrassed and shocked, I shrieked like a girl, "What are you thinking? Put your clothes on!"

Call me a passive agent if you like, but I turned and ran out the door. I took flight down three floors of stairs and got into my car, even locked the doors. Sitting there and catching my breath, I watched as the weirdo woman walked out of the building, got in her car parked on the other side of the lot and drove away. Talk about being blindsided? I closed the unit up and returned to my office reporting the incident to my broker. As I thought about it later I began to wonder if she was really even a woman because what I saw in that lewd moment sure did not look too attractive to this gal!

We All Scream For Ice Cream

My very first contract after I became a Realtor was done on New Year's Day. I showed a unit to some clients on New Year's Eve and they told me to write up an offer. What a great way to start both my career and the new year. I immediately phoned my broker and he agreed to meet me at the office next morning to walk me through the paperwork. The offer was for $750,000. I was pumped!

Later that day I got a call from my buyers. They had decided spending that kind of money on a place they would only use maybe one month a year was probably not a good idea. Since they already owned another property in Palm Beach, they realized it made no sense to purchase a second property. With all due consideration of my work for them over the holiday, they said they wanted me to understand how they agonized over cancelling. As a consolation, they said they would be sending me a small gift of their appreciation.

Next day at my office, there was an envelope waiting for me. I opened it to find five $5.00 coupons to the Ice Cream Club. Hmm, a $22,500 commission versus $25 in ice cream? I guess they could have just cancelled. I wanted to scream.

Amortized Over 100 Years?

I was working with a first time home buyer recently who was very eager to learn everything possible about the buying process. Since I used to be a school teacher, I enjoyed his inquisitive nature and was happy to educate him during our house hunting excursions.

One day he asked me to explain how an amortized loan was calculated. I told him that there was a mathematical formula used to establish the set monthly payment over a term of years, given a certain loan amount and fixed interest rate. I told him that the amount of principal and interest in each payment would change every month as the loan balance decreased, but the total monthly payment would always be the same.

He said he still didn't understand so I told him that as an example, I would use a $100,000 loan amount to demonstrate the concept. If his set monthly payment was $1,000, his first payment would be $999.00 for interest and $1.00 toward principal. His second payment would be $998.00 for interest and $2.00 toward principal reduction. In the third month, there would be $997.00 for interest and $3.00 on principal, and so forth each month until the loan was completely paid off. It seemed he understood the idea.

Several weeks later, we wrote an offer on a home that he was truly excited about. It was a coincidence that his loan was going to be exactly $100,000. The next day, the seller accepted his offer and I called my buyer to give him the good news. However, he was not happy at all. As a matter of fact, he told me he did not want to buy the house after thinking it over the night before. Naturally, I asked him what made him change his mind.

He said, "I thought about the amortized loan you explained to me and realized it will take me 100 years to pay the whole thing off! That would be crazy!"

I had to laugh mostly at myself for being such a poor teacher! I promptly provided him a thirty year amortized schedule so he could see the actual breakdown of principal and interest, and with that he went ahead and happily bought his first home. I assured him I wouldn't have bought the home either if it was going to take 100 years to pay off the amortized loan!

Striking Oil

A friend of mine owned a house that had oil heating. Because of escalating oil prices, she had a contract price for automatic refilling every other month. The system had several components that included two 250 gallon tanks that were located in the basement.

It seems the neighbors had recently installed a natural gas unit in their home. They boasted to my friend continually about the economy of their new system, contrasting it to the outdated oil method for heating. My friend, who could be easily swayed into doing almost anything, decided that she too wanted to have the more economical heating. So, she contracted with a gas company and had a new gas furnace put in. The contractor who did the work removed the old oil tanks from her basement as a courtesy accommodation.

The problem was that no one told the oil company to stop delivering oil. One day while my friend was away, they delivered the oil as usual using the filler pipe still located in her backyard. When she came home later, the smell of oil was permeating throughout the house. She was understandably confused, so she went to her basement to investigate. Lo and behold, she saw what was over 400 gallons of precious crude poured inches deep over the entire basement floor. So, she loaded up the truck and moved to Beverly…Hills, that is!

Ups And Downs

There is a unique oceanfront condo complex that I really love on the south end of my town. One special aspect of the place is that there are only twenty-four units in the project, intimate enough that people get to know their neighbors. It is a rich environment and ranks tops for quality of living. For some eighty percent of the owners though, the property serves as a vacation or second home. It is a quiet sanctuary, a respite from the hustle and bustle of life.

The unit I was showing one afternoon was the crème-de-la-crème! It had its own private elevator opening directly into the foyer of the apartment. There were no common hallways. With this showplace you had completely private access up to the third floor. The complex did not have a doorman, instead the building was secured by use of a keypad at the main entrance.

On this particular day, I had just finished showing my listing to a good looking young couple. They seemed quite enamored with the place and my instincts were telling me this was going to be their choice. I had another showing scheduled immediately following them so I deliberately left the lights on in the unit, with drapes and sliding balcony doors left open.

I entered the elevator with the clients to escort them on the ride down. The doors closed and I pushed the lobby button. The car moved slightly, then suddenly stopped. "Okay," I said. "Let's try another button here." Nothing. I pried at the door. No way. I opened the phone box, picked up the receiver. Dead. Tried cell phones. No reception. Cool-hand Luke here was beginning to feel pressure from a rising tide of panic. The wife began to huff. She started nervously chattering about her claustrophobic issues while the husband was stone-cold silent. I pulled the emergency alarm button and assured the clients someone would come to our rescue quickly. The alarm bell rang a deafening sound, agitating us all the more.

Common sense told me someone would save us, but in the back of my mind I knew there were very few people around to hear the emergency bell. Then I thought, my next client was to meet me downstairs shortly so surely he would hear the alarm and rescue us. There had to be hope for the hopeless! I kept repeating this positive revelation to my blank-faced clients, but the words did little to relieve their anxiety.

One hour and thirty minutes later, we were rescued by the local fire department. They said they had been called by a resident in the building who initially thought the alarm was a "test", but after going on for so long decided it might not be. Turns out the client I had hoped would save us never could have anyway. He did not have the code for the keypad at the entrance and obviously walked away from the complex that afternoon thinking his broker, me, had stood him up.

As it turns out, the whole ordeal was my fault…I suppose. My seller later lectured that by leaving the sliders open on the balcony, a vacuum was formed, sealing the doors closed on the elevator and preventing the car from moving. "I told you about that when you listed the unit for sale," my seller scolded. "I told you not to ever leave the sliders open when leaving the unit." I felt shamed and put down for my ignoramus conduct!

Now, I would never want to call someone a liar, especially one of my clients, but in this situation, would you NOT think information that vital would have been reiterated loud and clear when I scheduled the showings with him? Hey, girlfriend, it was brand new information to this broker - after the fact - that day.

End of story is that my clients did not buy the unit; I never heard from them again. I left numerous messages for the other buyer I missed while stranded in the elevator, sincerely apologizing with full explanation of what had happened to me, but never heard from him again either.

So hear me when I say, "Just like that elevator…such are the ups and downs of this business!"

The Vanishing Listing

It is just good real estate business to preview properties. I believe in the value of previewing, broker open houses and caravans. After all, how can you sell something if you have never seen it? How unprofessional is it to drive around with a prospect looking for a property you want to show, but you have no idea how to get there? This can add to the credibility gap and taint a prospect's confidence in you. You must be diligent and vigilant in the real estate business to earn the respect of prospects.

I had recently listed a cute little diner that was located on a small leased lot. It was a prefab-type building, complete with built-in appliances and furniture, and nicely placed in the center of the gravel parking area. The owner explained he had already closed his business and needed to sell quickly as he was moving out of state. I immediately went to work on a marketing plan. Contacting several dozen local and out of town restaurant owners and pitching the business opportunity, I invited them to view the property at an open house in two weeks. I was calling my event an "Open Kitchen" and feeling quite proud of myself for the clever marketing phrase. Ten restaurant owners confirmed with me to attend the 10:30 a.m. event.

On "Open Kitchen" day, I headed over early to unlock the diner and make sure everything was in good order before anyone arrived. I am vigilant and diligent, remember? As I pulled off the roadway and into the diner's parking area, for one split second I thought I was at the wrong place. I put my car in park and then reality sank in. The diner was gone. Nothing was there but the restaurant sign dangling on its post and a square block foundation where the diner used to be. I was stunned, staring at the vacant lot and hardly believing my eyes. Next thing I realized, the parking area was filling up with my guests. They must have thought I was pulling some sort of marketing prank because there was clearly no kitchen to open. The diner had simply vanished and with it, my credibility!

It turned out that the owner had fallen behind on his payments. The finance company made quick work the night before in dismantling the prefab structure, loading it up with all its diner contents and repossessing the property. My listing was gone.

I guess there were a couple of lessons to be learned. One, timing is everything. Maybe if I had held my Open Kitchen sooner a sale might have saved my listing and saved me a lot of face as well. Number two, and you might recall that old saying *buyers are liars*? Well, I'm here to tell you, I learned that *buyers are NOT THE ONLY liars*! I was not a happy Realtor the day my listing vanished.

The Case Of The
Disappearing Kitchen

Several years ago I was acting as the attorney for a brokerage that had a listing in North San Diego County. The property went under contract to sell and an escrow was opened. The brokerage was double ending the deal, but with two different agents, one representing the seller and one representing the buyer. The escrow was scheduled to close on a Friday after a lengthy 60 day period.

On Saturday afternoon I received a call from the seller informing me that the escrow did not close the day before as scheduled. This in itself was not unusual in the world of real estate. As a matter of fact, statistically most escrows do not close on their target dates despite all efforts. So at that point, I had little concern and said, "Don't worry, lots of escrow closings get delayed." However, he went further to explain that the buyer had in fact cancelled the escrow. With years of experience in real estate law, I knew this eleventh hour cancellation would likely put the buyer in default under the terms of the contract and thus a forfeiture of the earnest money deposit. "Escrows are sometimes cancelled even if the cancellation is not justified," I consoled, assuring him that any loss would be compensated if the buyer had in fact defaulted.

As I was beginning to realize my efforts to placate the matter were falling on deaf ears, the seller blurted out, "The kitchen is gone!" The kitchen is gone? Had this seller lost his mind from the pressure of a failed escrow? Was I not hearing him correctly? It was a ridiculous idea to say the kitchen was gone. Then he fleshed out the rest of the story.

When the buyer went into escrow, he had intended to remodel the kitchen of the home after he closed on the deal. Because it was to be a major remodel, he had been already signed a construction contract with a contractor so the work would start the day following the Friday closing. The contractor had entered the property numerous times using a hidden key at the vacant home, finalizing the remodel plans, taking measurements and with professional mastery, rechecking every detail for what was to be a hard and fast work schedule once the escrow closed.

The contractor, under pressure to start the project on schedule, arrived early Saturday morning. The strict timeline under his construction agreement was carved in stone for that start date and he fully intended to perform. The problem was that no one told the contractor the deal fell through on Friday. The workmen arrived on Saturday and proceeded to rip out all appliances and cabinets, stripping the kitchen completely down to four walls.

Now I understood. With some fast and furious phone calling, the legal issues were put on the table for everyone involved to consider. With more than a bit of squirming over that weekend, a practical solution was found and by Monday morning we had established a new game plan.

Amazingly the story had a fairly happy ending. The buyer forfeited their earnest deposit voluntarily, my client kicked in some money and we found a contractor who installed a much improved kitchen for a reasonable price. The seller was able to raise the price based on the new kitchen and sold to a new buyer. Because my client acted so quickly and responsibly, the broker-

The Case Of The Disappearing Kitchen

age was able to keep the listing and recoup a portion of the loss with a commission from the new sale. I can only imagine the seller's dismay on that Saturday when he discovered his kitchen had disappeared.

Has Anyone Seen Our Garage?

The young couple had been married for five years, pinching pennies for a down payment and waiting to start a family until they bought their first home. You can imagine how excited they were when they finished their final walk thru and the inspection was flawless. Their anticipation grew even stronger as they drove to the attorney's office next morning for the closing. For them, it was a dream come true and the beginning of a new chapter in their lives.

With keys in hand, they headed to the house to meet the movers who were waiting for them in the driveway. A group of welcoming neighbors were there too with balloons and some homemade cookies for the event. Everyone was on board to help the proud little first time homeowners move in.

Only something was missing when they got there. The garage was gone. No sign of it anywhere. It had been there the day before. The seller still had two antique cars parked in it then, but it was gone now without a trace. No garage, no cars. Nothing but a pea gravel square where it had been last seen.

Who do you call? The police? A lawyer? The couple was dumbfounded and finally decided to call their agent. When the agent arrived, he was equally confused and the sparks began to fly! The agent called the broker who then called the seller. The seller in fact had the garage, but the problem was the seller had no intention of giving it back. He claimed it was never part of the sale because it was not a permanent structure, obviously portable and not anchored down. The seller put the monkey square on his broker's back saying he had told the broker it was personal property when he listed the house. It was not part of the deal.

Both the broker and the agent became scapegoats in the debacle, even though the broker insisted he had no knowledge of the garage being excluded. So, rather than risk a lawsuit, the two Realtors pooled their commission money and replaced the missing garage. Sound familiar, fellow agents?

Lost And Found

I am a single lady who has been a licensed Realtor for six years. I have developed a good referral business over the years, working directly with national and international relocation departments. I recently received an inbound referral for a couple being transferred to my city from Barcelona, Spain.

The couple with their three children had just made the tiring flight from Europe that morning and checked into a day-to-day, furnished rental with the expectation of purchasing a townhouse before their furniture shipment arrived from Spain. They required that the complex be child friendly with a minimum of three bedrooms and two full baths. The only possible match in their price range just happened to have two units available for sale. We met at the complex with high hopes of getting them quickly into a place that their young children could call home.

We walked through a lovely courtyard to view the first townhome. Anna carried her little nine month old in a pouch carrier across her chest while Doug held the hands of his other two children, ages six and three. We entered the first unit that was beautifully furnished, but with near white carpeting throughout. The couple was concerned that the light colored carpeting would not work with the children. Locking up and heading to the next unit, I explained this townhouse was occupied by a family same size as theirs and most likely more suited for children.

We were greeted at the door by the wife. She suggested letting the children watch TV in the upstairs den with hers while the parents looked around, but only three year old Damian took the offer. His older sister who spoke little English was too shy to leave her father's side. My clients were serious about this unit. Anna and Doug talked with the owner at length, discussing all the details of area schools, activities and such that a newcomer would need to know. I felt the deal was pretty much sealed by the time we left.

Anna and Doug agreed it was their choice. They were ready to write their offer immediately and finalize the purchase as quickly as possible. As we rushed along back to the parking lot, I continued explaining the buying process to them and we agreed to meet at my office in fifteen minutes to prepare the paperwork. They didn't want to risk another buyer coming in with a competing offer. Our cars were parked side by side, and I was just pulling away when Anna and Doug began screaming wildly at me.

"Stop, stop. We've left Damian!" Doug was flushed and panicky. In an instant I realized that we had completely forgotten little Damian. Doug and I raced back to the townhouse, both of us pretty embarrassed that something like this could have happened, and there was Damian fast asleep on the couch in front of the TV. Not even the owner realized the quiet little Spanish boy was still there.

When Doug picked him up, Damian looked at his dad all sleepy-eyed and not knowing he had been left behind, then asked, "Papa, is this going to be our new b-b-brownhouse?"

The little fella misunderstood the word townhouse. His dad said yes and layed his head over his shoulder where he immediately fell back to sleep.

It was such a sweet moment, I thought I was going to cry.

Circumstantial Evidence

When I was Vice President of Marketing with a major real estate company, putting out fires on listing complaints was part of my job. One day I received a call from an irate seller who had only recently listed her home with our agency.

She came on like gangbusters! Screaming at the top of her lungs, she was literally flipping out and threatening in no uncertain terms, "I will have your agent arrested! I will have his license and press charges against you too!"

"Madam…" I tried to interject.

But not listening at all, she harangued over me even louder, "When I came home just now I found your agent's card, and my fur coat is missing!"

I took a d-e-e-e-p breath and calmly said, "If our agent took your coat, do you really think he would have left his card for you?" And with that, she slammed the receiver in my ear. Ouch!

Moral of the story? It's always the Realtor's fault.

Wrong Number

I recently showed a condominium to a client who I had been working with for what seemed like forever. It was located in one of the upscale Trump buildings. The listing agent was an older gentleman named Frank who must have been well into his eighties. I had never had the pleasure of working with him before, but since my client was very interested it looked likely that Frank and I would be developing a new business relationship.

My client had a number of questions, however, before he was willing to extend an offer on the unit. He wanted to know about the association's reserve fund and when the most recent major assessment had been made. Clarifying the number of parking spaces with the unit and a few other specific details regarding building construction would give my client a complete picture to formulate a purchase contract.

I called Frank to get the information so that I could respond to my client's questions. On each question I asked, Frank would say, "I don't know. The manager would have to answer that one." At the end of our conversation, I said to Frank, "So, you'll get back to me with those answers?" His reply, "No. Here's the manager's number. You can call him yourself."

When I hung up the phone, I was a little more than annoyed with his lack of helpfulness. What kind of a listing agent is this who doesn't know the details of his property and who can't be bothered to get the information when asked? It seemed as if he could really have cared less.

But not looking to pick any fights, I complied and phoned the manager myself who answered all of my questions. I was prepared now to call my client and provide him with the information. When he answered, I poured right into my report, "I have all the answers to your questions since the other broker was of no help whatsoever and didn't know anything about his listing. I mean, how unprofessional do you have to be to take a high end listing and not know anything about what you're selling. I mean for a guy his age, he should know better, and if he doesn't care enough, he shouldn't be selling real estate." This rant to my client was a soothing vent of my annoyance toward Frank.

I waited for my client to respond, but there was a long uncomfortable silence. The person on the other end of the phone finally answered, "I think you dialed the wrong person. This is Frank, the incompetent listing agent."

I was so embarrassed with myself and completely lost for words. I had called the agent by mistake instead of my client. In that terrible moment, I said, "Oh, sorry. I must have the wrong number," and hung up fast.

Although I presented an offer to Frank shortly thereafter, surprisingly it was not accepted and no counter offer was ever presented back to me. Needless to say, I never heard from Frank again.

Why Do I Have To Sell My House?

In 1985 working as a Realtor was different in some ways from today. One difference was that we did not use computers. Each month the Board of Realtors published a book that contained all of the listings. It was the size of a telephone directory. In it were all the active listings as of the first of the month. In the back were the solds and expireds from the previous month. Agents had to fax or hand deliver a form directly to the Board of all listing details for the monthly publication, and if there was a photo included, the quality was very poor. There were a lot of typos that led to mix-ups and mistakes.

Another difference was that most associations did not use keysafes. If you were planning to show clients eight houses on a Saturday, that meant going to eight different listing agencies and checking out the key. When you were done at the end of the day, you had to return all of them. It made for a long day, and I still believe more than a few prospects bought one of the eight out of sheer exhaustion.

I remember one incident back then when I was principal broker and one of my agents had checked out a key from a cooperating office. He proceeded to the house with the customer following in his car. Arriving at the property, my agent noted that there was no "For Sale" sign in the yard, so he knocked deliberately, loudly and repeatedly on the front door. There was no answer.

There were no sounds, no one stirring about, no barking dogs, no reason not to enter. He put the key into the lock and the door swung open easily. It was already unlocked.

Upon entering the home, he began to wonder if he was in the right house. He looked at the listing in his big old book, but none of the detailed information seemed to match that address and there was no picture to compare. When just about then, a gentleman, dressed only in his boxers, came out from a rear bedroom. The man was barely awake and seemed puzzled seeing the agent there. He asked, "What are you doing in my house?"

My agent identified himself and said, "I'm here to try to sell your house."

The groggy homeowner nodded affirmatively, and after several moments asked, "Why do I have to sell my house?"

Although real estate technology has changed over the years, the funny mix-ups back then are no different than what can happen today - wrong house! And another thing that will never change in our profession - the people! That's what makes it so much fun!

Failure To Launch

Maybe you've seen the movie about the adult son who was still living at home with his parents and didn't want to move out? A couple of years back, I had some clients who wanted to sell their rental home where their adult son had been living for years - and not paying any rent. My clients were at their wits' end with the freeloading young man and decided selling the place was the only way to get him out on his own. The clients gave me their son's phone number, keys to the house and a warning to expect resistance.

The freeloader was very uncooperative with me and to make the matter worse, he had two vicious dogs. These were the kind of dogs with drool dripping from their chops and big, sharp teeth! Seriously, they were dangerous animals.

I had a showing appointment and begged the son to please tie up the dogs. When I got there, he was gone and the dogs were loose in the yard. The beastly canines ran at the fence, ferociously barking as we approached the house. It practically scared my client to death, but I insisted we would get the matter handled. I was determined that the son's plot to keep me at bay so the house would never sell was not going to work!

My eight year old son just happened to be with me and I asked him to wait with my client in her car while I ran to the corner market. I bought dog biscuits and returned. Next I had my son climb onto the roof of the little detached outbuilding next to the fence. He threw biscuits in through the open door to bait the dogs. It worked! He then used a broomstick from overhead to push the shed door closed. Ha!

I was able to access the property, show the home and made the sale! The freeloading son was finally launched into adulthood, packing those intimidating dogs along with him.

Don't Shoot The Messenger

My seller of a duplex wanted an "As Is" sale, but agreed that we could do a home inspection. He told me he would leave a key for the vacant unit under the front door mat. He explained the tenant in the left unit would not be home because he was in jail, and he'd put the key for that unit under its front door mat as well. He gave no explanation why the tenant was in jail and I didn't ask.

The other agent and I arrived early to open up both sides. When we found no key under the mat for the left unit, I started feeling some pressure. The inspector and buyers would be arriving shortly. The buyer's agent then began whining that her clients had taken the day off from work for the appointment and threatened it was not going to go over well if she had to reschedule everyone to complete the inspection on another day.

Determined to keep the show moving forward, I eyed the partially open window to the living room of the locked unit. "Not a problem," I announced, "I'll climb in."

So just that easily, I slid the window up and leaned over. Head first, I was going in. Just as my hands and forehead touched the floor inside, my legs still laid out over the sill, I heard the gruffest voice shout, "Where in the #!^#^!# do you think you're going?"

Standing to the side of me was a man in jockey shorts and holding a gun. My seller's jailbird tenant was obviously home now.

With the guy towering over me, I was hardly able to cough up the words, "Oh…we're having the home inspection today."

The other agent, waiting like an innocent bystander outside, must have heard his scary voice. Her mousy whisper, "Are you okay, Irene?" was no backup at all. I had a feeling she was inching away and ready to run for her life, abandoning me to fend for myself in that compromised position. But, I stood myself up and explained my way into the guy's good graces. He didn't shoot me.

Lesson learned: Don't believe sellers and NEVER climb in a window.

When It Rains, It Pours

Did you ever have a transaction that was just meant to be? In spite of every conceivable obstacle, the buyer still wanted to purchase the property? This doesn't happen very often, but it's a nice surprise when it does.

I had a client who I'd been working with for weeks. One morning I took her and her children out to look at more homes. The first house we stopped at was brand new on the market. The listing agent told me there was a key in the lockbox and the owners would not be home. We pulled up and went inside for a tour. It was love at first sight and my customer was thrilled as it was just what she had been looking for. I told her I had scheduled several other properties to show her, and although she didn't want to see any more homes, she agreed to go because the appointments had already been arranged. She reluctantly left her dream house to go with me.

About two hours later and after viewing four other homes, she was still set on the first house. I asked if she was ready to make an offer and she was, but wanted to take one more look so we headed back to the dream house. On the way there the sky began to cloud-up and a light drizzle of rain quickly turned into an outright downpour. When we arrived at the house, I told my client to wait in the car with the kids while I ran first to get the door open. I grabbed my attache' and made a dash for the front door. She then gathered her children and they quickly splashed across the driveway and into the house. After revisiting all the rooms and considering its suitability for her family, she was ready to write her offer. We sat at the dining table to start the paperwork.

While sitting there with us, her six year old daughter asked to use the restroom. I said of course. The little girl had been gone for maybe five minutes before returning to the table in dripping wet clothes. Naturally her mother asked what had happened and she explained it was raining in the bathroom. "Raining in the bathroom?" mom and I mimicked in harmony, then ran to the bathroom.

The minute I looked in my heart dropped as I knew this would be a deal breaker. There was water literally draining through the ceiling light fixture just above the toilet. Now what are the chances of that happening at the exact moment you're writing up an offer to purchase? Rattled as I was by this, I told my buyer not to worry because we could do a home inspection to see what was wrong. My client seemed perfectly okay with that.

Back to the table to complete her paperwork, and I was again interrupted. There was someone ringing the doorbell, repeatedly. I looked out the front window and there was a truck parked in the driveway that read "Critter Control."

"Oh my Lord," I thought. "Now what?"

When I opened the door, there was a man decked out like a hunter. He had on a camouflage zip-up suit and brimmed hat that had a netted veil tucked into his collar. He was carrying two animal cages. He had arrived, he proudly and loudly announced, to take care of the bat problem in the attic! I asked if he was sure he was at the right place and after double-checking his work order, he was. Off to the attic he went.

I thought to myself, "Who would buy a house that was taking in more water than the Titanic and Batman in the attic?"

My client didn't even flinch over the critter guy's entrance before insisting that we finish her offer. We included a roof inspection and bat remediation as contingencies, and the deal ultimately came together at a reduced price. My client can't wait to move into her dream home. Go figure!

It Was A Crashing Good Closing

I am a professional Realtor and would like to say with humility that over the years I have learned a lot. Someone once told me that it is not how many years a broker has been in the business, but how many transactions they have closed that warrants any badge of honor. If I can toot my own horn a bit, I have won some pretty prestigious Realtor Of The Year awards during my stint in this business for gross closed sales. If you are impressed with my credentials, thank you. I try to present myself at all times as intelligent and composed. I have prided myself especially with the ability to stay calm in the midst of real estate storms. Some would say I am cool, calm and collected no matter what.

Several years ago I was working with a wealthy client who was looking for a luxury home to purchase in a particular suburb. Over a period of several months, I proposed a number of properties to him and finally found the perfect place. The client was an executive for a large corporation. He lived with a demanding work schedule, so I knew it was very important to make every phone call with him exacting, getting quickly to the point. It was nothing but business, short and sweet between him and me.

The contract to purchase was negotiated and every step of the transaction was handled with perfection on my part. There were no surprises and no disappointments along the way, but for one small issue. The owner of the home was also a busy businessman and his moving-out schedule was one day overlapping with my client's moving-in schedule. In discussing this conflict with the seller's agent, we were finally able to agree to a very small window of time for the transition. On closing day, the seller would have to be completely moved out by noon and the buyer could start moving in by one o'clock. The challenge was in making sure that both parties' moving companies could accommodate this strict schedule. All agreed, we then arranged the closing to be held at the subject property during the hour between those two events.

At 11:30 that day, the entire closing party of people were ready to finalize the transaction and we congregated around the kitchen island. There were files and papers scattered everywhere as both buyer and seller studied their final documents to be signed. The seller's moving crew had the house cleaned out now except for the attic. Gathered in the kitchen, it was somewhat of a distraction with thumping and bumping noises overhead as the movers labored to haul out the last of the seller's stored belongings up there.

When suddenly, like a strike of lightening, the ceiling above the kitchen island broke open. A guy dropped onto the island with a thunderous crash, pouring drywall, dust and insulation over everything. I got the worst of the cloudburst when a piece of insulation rained down on my head and drooped over my face. But worse than how I looked at that moment was the way I reacted. I completely lost my professional self. I mean I lost it! The words that flew out of my mouth in that startling moment are things not fit for print, things even a crazy, drunken sailor wouldn't rant in public. I jumped and flung my arms around like a panicked cuckoo bird.

After a few more expletives, everyone began to regain some semblance of composure, especially me. We could see the guy was not hurt, just overwhelmed. He had been straddling the joists in the attic to move boxes and lost his balance, unavoidably stepping onto the insulation and ceiling drywall. With that, down he came. That is just what happened.

Now with major ceiling damage, our closing had to be delayed until the moving company's insurance company took care of the claim several days later. We then closed the deal and my client took possession of his beautiful home. He was very happy with my service, but I am afraid my reputation for being cool, calm and collected as a professional has been marred since that crashing closing.

My Sale Still Had Traction

A number of years ago I had a house listed that was on a hill with a steep driveway. I got a sign call from a retired couple who wanted to see the home. I was thrilled for the appointment opportunity because it was the middle of January, snow on the ground, and the slowest time of year for house sales in my area.

Eager to meet them and make my best presentation, I arrived early and drove right up the snow covered driveway with no problem. The couple arrived in their truck and had no problem with traction, parking next to my car on the landing in front of the garage.

The couple absolutely fell in love with the home and as we were revisiting all the rooms, their daughter-in-law arrived, parking behind the couple's truck. Minutes later their son arrived and parked behind his wife. After a short family discussion, the couple wanted to make an offer so I started filling out the contract for them in the kitchen. When all of the sudden their son yelled, "Oh, noooo!"

Looking out the front window we saw that the son's car had slid down the drive and into a snow piled ditch at the street. Quickly putting on his coat, hat and gloves and heading out the door ahead of the rest of us to survey any possible damage, he yelled out again, even louder, "Oh, no! No! No!" and he took off running. I flew out the door behind him just in time to see his wife's car slowly sliding backwards down the driveway and then, bang! The back of it crashed right into the front of her husband's car, pushing it even further into the ditch. Both the front of his car and the back of her's were smashed.

The buyer wife and I stood shivering on the landing looking down at the scene. I felt awful! Then the sweet wife put her arm around me and said, "Don't worry, honey. We're still going to buy the house."

And they did.

The Cops Sealed My Deal

This is one story in my real estate career I will never forget! It had to do with a listing I had near the 10 Freeway in LA about ten years ago. It was located in what I knew to be a high crime neighborhood.

I met a client and her young son at the vacant home at 4 o'clock on a Friday afternoon. When I tried to open the combination key box on the side door, it was jammed and no matter how I tried, I couldn't get it to open. Since I had driven across town for the appointment, I was not about to leave before getting into the property to show it. The client continued to patiently wait, but persistent as I was, the box wouldn't open.

Finally, I decided to go to the neighbor's house and see if I could get some "manly" help. The neighbor guy was a very husky Hispanic gentleman and when I explained the problem, he agreed to come over with a few tools. He couldn't get the key box open either, so we decided to remove some of the inserts from the louvered windows in the back of the house to get in. He made quick work of that and gave me a boost through the opening.

Now inside, I unlocked the side door and invited my waiting buyer in. I asked the neighbor if he would be good enough to remove the doorknob with the jammed key box so I could take it with me when I left and he said it would be no problem. So while he was working on the side door, I gave my client a tour of the house.

Not more than ten minutes had gone by when I heard a loudspeaker blaring, "Whoever's in the house, come out with your hands up!"

I opened the front door and we all stepped out onto the porch. There were four policemen with their guns drawn. It scared the daylights out of us! I mean, it was VERY scary! I asked the officers if I could put my hands down and then explained who I was and what had happened. Thank goodness, they believed me. They put their guns down and actually apologized for scaring us. I was shocked.

While still at the property, I then got a call from my out of state clients who owned the home. They were very upset because they had been called and alerted of a possible break in at their vacant home. I told them the story.

My prospect was so impressed with the Neighborhood Watch and the way the police handled the situation, she called the next day to say she wanted to make an offer and ended up purchasing the house. In my twenty years in real estate, I've yet to hear of another agent with a story like this.

Persistence In The Face Of Adversity

I was awarded Rookie of the Year in 2008. I arrived at my brokerage determined to make a big splash in the real estate world and was all full of myself with smarts and determination. Aside from my driving work ethic, one particular transaction that year was in large part why I received the award.

I inherited a thirty-two property package to sell in which all the properties were in default and dilapidated. Short selling them would be the only option. All the properties had at least two bank liens and had been purchased sight unseen by a grandfather/grandson duo of investors from California. Due to the number of properties and complexity of managing what had turned into a mess, I had to meet weekly with their six attorneys to give status reports.

On one of these properties, my team had successfully negotiated the short sale and agreed sale price with the lenders before I had a buyer. The agreed shortage was so low on this 4-plex that it quickly became my hottest listing. The fact that the property had a ton of deferred maintenance and was basically falling apart was a huge motivation in the bank agreeing to the fire sale, low pricing. They also acknowledged it was located in a very rough neighborhood which made for high risk holding.

READY, WILLING & (unbeliev)ABLE

It was a hot, Texas summer day, temperatures in the low 100's when I drove out to show the property to two investor partners. When they arrived, it was obvious to me that they were excited about the rental income/price ratio. Looking around the outside of the 4-plex, they seemed comfortable with its condition, deteriorated as it was.

We then proceeded to gather the keys from the hidden lock box to begin looking inside the individual units one at a time. At Unit No. 1, a small child answered the door, barely cracking it open to let us know her parents were not home and to come back later. Understanding that, we went next to Unit No. 2. I knocked on the door. Suddenly the door was hit from the inside by what sounded like a pack of pit bull dogs. The door actually bulged outward as they slammed against it from the inside; their ferocious barking and growling made the three of us step back quickly. Needless to say, we were not going to go inside that unit today. On to door No. 3. A nice young lady opened her door and was willing to show us her unit. I noted near the door, the cold air return was completely clogged with cat hair while the A/C ran constantly. The temperature needle was pegged at 65 degrees and the rooftop compressor was condensating so badly that water was steadily dripping through the ceiling and down the wall.

At this point, I was not feeling so confident about being able to sell this 4-plex. The investors had told me they needed to see at least two of the units to make a decision or maintain any interest, so I pressed on to door No. 4. I made an on-purpose decision to project to these buyer prospects a positive vibration in spite of the scary scene thus far. I imagined some cosmic force could flow from me to cause them to be undaunted by this unfolding disappointment of a mess. I was determined to persevere.

Unit No. 4 was unoccupied so I unlocked the door and we entered. I locked the door behind us as a matter of safety since we were in such a bad ghetto neighborhood. At once we smelled a strong odor of urine. It was noxious enough that we had to cover our faces, pulling our shirt collars over our noses. We could hear from the next room a yapping little dog just carrying on something terrible. Looking in the bedroom, there was an abandoned bed and mattress. It was covered with food scraps and doggy poop. There was trash everywhere and the most angry Chihuahua I have ever seen. He hopped up on the food stained bed, barking incessantly trying to frantically stare us down. That dog suddenly started to pee for what seemed like an eternity. He peed on the mattress, the clothing strewn about and kept on peeing in his frenzy.

Sweat pouring off my brow due to the heat in the unit, I was about to give up the effort to look any farther when suddenly there was loud yelling and screaming at the front door. Someone was banging the door and next thing I knew a man came busting through accusing us of breaking into his home. He pushed me back as I tried desperately not to fall down on that filthy floor. The clients stood him back and we were finally able to make him understand who we were and why we were there. Just about then, the crazy Chihuahua ran out the open front door and the man went back into a fit yelling at us for letting his dog get loose. It was a terrible disaster in front of my buyer prospects, but I was able to finally settle the insanity enough to get myself and the clients out the door safely.

If short sales are not hard enough, try surviving the challenge I had in attempting to show those four units! Despite the odors, the dogs and the crazy-making, a good deal is a good deal and those investors ended up buying the 4-plex. The moral of the story from this Rookie of the Year is that hard work and persistence can pay off in the face of adversity.

Flea Flicker

I had an appointment with a buyer named Sandy to show a nice listing of mine. My seller had already moved out of the home, taking her personal belongings and beloved pack of dogs, four of them, to her new place. She had agreed to leave much of her furniture behind for staging the place while it was being marketed.

Arriving early at the vacant property, I wanted to make sure all was in order since the seller's move-out several days earlier. Inside, I was happy to see she left everything well arranged. After opening the shutters and turning on all the lights, I sat down on the couch to wait for Sandy to arrive for the showing. Reviewing the buyer folder I had prepared for her, I looked over the printout of neighborhood comps to refresh my memory, then clipped my card to the color brochure of the listing and set it neatly on the coffee table. I was ready for my client to arrive.

Not quite! As I leaned back to relax, crossing my leg comfortably, I noticed a bunch of brown specs on the pant leg of my khakis. "What the heck is that?" I sat up and started to flick the specs off when I realized they were fleas, thousands of them! I was infested with them and they seemed to be multiplying by the second, a swarming mass moving up the legs of my pants aiming in a direction I did NOT like! Struck with panic, I jumped off the couch and dropped my trousers right there. Overwhelmed with the creeps, I kicked off my shoes, hopping one-footed to pull off my socks quick as I could. In desperation I yanked my tie, catapulting it and my shirt to the other side of the room. Freak out of all freak outs! Down to my boxers and barefoot, I bolted out the front door, grabbing my keys and wallet on the way. This tenderfoot would have volunteered to run over hot coals to get to the safety of his car in that moment.

And who do you think I bumped smack dab into as I slammed the door closed behind me? "Sandy! House can't be shown. Sorry. Must go! I will call you. Sorry." And I was gone.

I stood in the hot shower at home for over half an hour before the heebie-jeebies were finally gone. It was then that I phoned Sandy to tell her what happened and that my seller was going to have to fumigate the house for fleas before it could be shown. She couldn't stop laughing as she described what I looked like in my skivvies, skedaddling out of there, leaving dust behind as I sped down the street.

Weeks later I went back to show the house. All the fleas were gone, but my clothes were still there, strewn across the room right where I left them that day.

Flea For All

Back in May of 1996, my friend was showing a lady customer some of his houses. The two of them were very flirty with each other the first few times they went out looking. It was pretty obvious the flames of passion were beyond the kindling stage when they met one day at a vacant house.

There in the kitchen they started going at it. Their carnal desires led them to the living room floor where they ... well, you know. After they were done in the living room, they got dressed, finished previewing the house and left in his car. But it wasn't more than a block down the street when he began itching, then she began itching.

He noticed what looked like a knat on his arm as he was driving along. When he took a swat at the annoyance, it didn't fly and he realized it was a flea. Just about then she looked down at her black boots and noticed they were peppered with little brownish dots - that were moving - and she shrieked. He pulled the car over and they both jumped out. There was a frenzy of jumping and tugging as he threw off his golf shirt and she pitched her boots.

Emotionally rattled, they got back in the car and he drove straight to the next house they had intended to look at where they found private seclusion in the basement. They stripped off the rest of their clothes and thoroughly checked each other for signs of any fleas. The car had to be treated with flea spray and I couldn't...I mean, my friend couldn't get the smell out for weeks.

The Unwelcomed Visitor

I was preparing to do an open house on Kristen Lane in our prestigious lakefront community. This was new construction and as the house had been closed up all week, the air inside was stuffy when I got there. I turned on the A/C and opened the double front doors. I arranged my guestbook and pens on a small table in the foyer then brought in a beautiful arrangement of fresh flowers which I placed nearby. Opening all the plantation shutters to just the right angle, I then laid out my beautiful color brochures along the bottom step of the winding staircase. It looked inviting with the huge double doors open and my pretty welcome table at the entry.

I headed to the kitchen to make freshly brewed coffee and wiped off the granite counters and sink. As I was placing cups and napkins on the kitchen island, I heard a faint noise in the direction of the front door so I called out, "Hello, come on in," thinking it was my first guest of the day.

When I heard no response, I left the kitchen and walked into the front room. "What?" I wondered, seeing my brochures scattered about the floor and my flowers strewn here and there as well. "What the heck happened here?" I was completely baffled at the mess in the foyer.

Just then a couple came walking up the entryway to the house. I greeted them and as we stood in the foyer, I began apologizing for the mysterious muddle I had just discovered. Then, like an emergency siren, the woman screamed, "Ooooh, my gosh!" On the opposite side of the living room was a giant white crane that had wandered into the house. It was nervously looking about and eyeing the front doorway when it suddenly spread its five foot wingspan and took to flight! It soared around the great room with aviator precision before flying out the front doors as we ducked and covered. Passing over, the darn bird left a large deposit that splattered on the tiled entry only inches from where I cowered.

Is it any wonder we agents don't like those lookie-loos who wander into our open houses and then fly out the door leaving a bogus calling card behind?

Business Went To The Dogs

Several years ago, my girlfriend and I were out for dinner with friends and I was asked how the real estate market was holding up. I told them that it seemed to be slowing down and getting harder to make a sale. "Overall," I said, "it has become a doggy dog struggle!" I had an epiphany. When we got home, I ran the idea past my girlfriend. Her first response was to say I must have had one too many drinks at the restaurant, but I persisted. "I'm serious about this," I said. "Since the real estate market has slowed down, how about if we look to sell homes to a different clientele? ... Dogs!"

After researching the market and finding that the dog market was a billion dollar industry, I was even more driven to pursue the idea. It just made sense that with my experience selling high end homes to high end customers, I could make the business venture successful. I would sell high end doggie homes for all the pampered pups of my high end clientele. I convinced my girlfriend to get on board with her crazy-and-genius boyfriend's idea. Doggie Mansions came into being.

Our first house was to be donated to the March of Dimes auction. The event was to be a charity dinner at the Ritz Carlton and we knew there would be hundreds of high end people there. It would be the perfect way to showcase our new product. We hired ome builder, who was currently otherwise out of work, and four weeks later our first Doggie Mansion was unveiled.

It was a Country Estate with seventy-five square feet of living space, the equivalent of five hundred square feet of human space. The amenities included Saturnia Italian marble floors, sheet rocked walls, electricity, flat screen television and, of course, air conditioning. The windows and doors were made of impact glass. The video and audio components came stocked with the most popular canine music and shows. Our interior decorator found magnificent furniture, specially treated for the pet resident, and the attached summer porch was a perfect finishing touch for the masterpiece.

To say that our Country Estate was anything short of a hit at the auction would be an understatement. Word of our new residential pet housing product spread quickly throughout town and across the country. The phones began ringing and the orders arrived! We had to hire an architect to design several more mansion styles. Some of the big sellers were the trendy Malibu Beach Mansion, the extraordinary Brick Tudor and the Mediterranean Villa, complete with tile roof and hardwood flooring.

We had a lovely run with the business for about a year. During that time we were featured on Animal Planet and ABC's 20/20 which boosted our sales volume even more. Our special Realtor's referral program proved to be highly successful in generating sales. The program targeted home buyers who wanted a Doggie Mansion that was a replica of their new home. The innovative idea made network television.

As the real estate market began heading more in the direction of a nosedive, we decided to shut down manufacturing on the Doggie Mansions even though we were still getting requests for celebrity sales. We decided that the opulence of $10,000-$25,000 dog houses was not an image we wanted to support during a time when people were losing their homes in the rash of foreclosures and short sales.

It is our vision, however, that once the economy comes back and people are financially sound, dogs will again be living the good life in their custom Doggie Mansions.

The Runaway Dog

Bill, an agent in my office, recently showed his listing to a prospective buyer. The home had just come on the market, and Bill was really excited at the thought of possibly double ending the million dollar sale.

When he arrived at the property, he rang the doorbell to make sure nobody was home as he thought. Using his private set of keys to the house, he opened the door into the kitchen. When quick as a flash a dog ran out between his legs and down the driveway. It was a medium sized dog, maybe a cocker spaniel, and Bill was taken completely by surprise. He had no idea the family owned a dog but knew he had to catch it and get it back.

Embarrassed by the unforeseen circumstance, Bill asked his buyers if they could reschedule since he had to retrieve the family's pet. They promptly left in their car so that he could get on the pursuit. Bill relocked the door and headed toward the street.

The temperature that day was well over ninety degrees and Bill slung his sport coat over his shoulder as he picked up his stride looking in every direction for the mutt. Some ten blocks up the street, Bill heard dogs barking and growling. It sounded like a squabble going on. Dripping with sweat, he rounded the side of a house and spotted the escapee going at it nose to nose with two dogs inside their fenced yard. Bill got hold of its collar and picked the spaniel up, but realized it was way too heavy to carry so he pulled off his belt to make a leash. Dragging the dog along, he was finally able to put it back in the house and retired to his car. His sport coat was ruined, he was wet and covered with dog hair and overall agitated by the disaster. He was worried he might even lose the prospective buyers he sent away earlier.

Later that evening, Bill was stepping out to meet a friend for dinner. His cell rang and when he answered, it was Paul, the owner of the home. Paul was short and to the point, "Hey, Bill, do me a favor. Rip up the listing agreement we signed last week. I don't want you in my f---- house anymore. Do you think it's funny what you did today?"

Really set back, Bill asked, "What are you talking about?"

"Why did you lock up a dog in my house? Do you have any idea what that damn dog did to my house? I'm going to have to hire a cleaning crew just to get my house back in shape. And guess who's going to get the f---- bill?" The phone went dead.

As you can imagine, Bill was rattled. He had started his day thinking he was going to double end a million dollar deal and now had nothing. His client hung up on him and his listing was gone. He excused himself from the dinner and headed to home feeling confused and discouraged. He was beginning to doubt his own sanity in the midst of this head scratching craziness!

Then his phone rang. It was Paul. With trepidation Bill answered and Paul began, "Hey, Bill, I'm so sorry about my last phone call. There has been a huge mix up here and I owe you a big apology. My grandson who's been visiting had been hiding a stray dog in his bedroom unbeknownst to us. We had no idea. Of course we want you to continue marketing the house for us if you will."

Oh sigh of relief! Now the craziness made a little more sense. Just earlier, contemplating a career change seemed like the only sane and stable decision for Bill to make, but the apology got his feet back under him. Now he knew he wasn't nuts - but he's still not ruling out a career change.

Nice Doggy

In the years before the advent of iPhones, Blackberries, wireless internet laptops and texting, I was out showing property to a young couple. We drove past a home with a for sale sign that was not on my printout and they asked if they could see it. I did the only thing an aggressive agent in those days would do with a hot buyer in hand, I went to the door unannounced and knocked. There was no answer.

I discovered a lock box on the railing and while my clients were still waiting in the car, decided to take my chances and go in to look around. Just that quickly I heard a growl that backed me up against the closed front door. It was a German shepherd and she was showing her teeth! I broke out into a cold sweat, certain that a terrible thing was about to happen to me when out of my mouth came, "SIT!" To my great relief, she obeyed. I decided to put the dog in the backyard.

Taking her by the collar, I pulled the drapes back from the sliding glass door. Just as I started to open the slider an even larger German shepherd from outside took a fierce, barking leap toward me. It's head actually got squeezed in the slider as I tried to defend myself, until finally the big male pulled back. Then I quickly shoved the other dog out. Now I could safely call my clients to come inside and give them the tour. Sad to say, they didn't like the home at all, and I had gone through all of that for naught!

But that was not the worst of it…the next day I received a call from my Board of Realtors office informing me that a complaint had been lodged against me by the owners of the dogs. It seems they were show dogs and were expressly kept apart so they wouldn't breed. I innocently put them together. It wasn't until a month later that the complaint was dropped when it was confirmed that there was no doggie pregnancy.

In today's world, I could have called the listing agent by cell or at least accessed the MLS to find out if there were any special showing instructions, but not back then, kids! It was a stressful lesson learned.

Dog House For Sale

I am a licensed Realtor who works in Hawaii. Over the years in my business, I have sold all types of homes. On the top end of my list was a fabulous plantation property with Lanai room, bamboo flooring, vaulted ceilings and coastline views. It sold in the millions. Most of my sales, however, have been mid-priced homes and condos. Of course in Hawaii even those are considered island jewels.

A former client called one day to say he had been watching a certain property on his street that had been going into disrepair for years. A For Sale sign had just been put up and he was interested in seeing the inside. He knew the owner in passing and warned me that the eccentric resident was believed to be a dog hoarder. No one on the street knew for sure just how many dogs he had behind the privacy hedges that lined the front of his property. But knowing my client's neighborhood to be quite nice, I took his recitation to be tainted with an air of snobbery. I dressed in my usual professional way, an expensive dress and heels, and met him at the place.

As we passed through the front gate, my client handed me a handkerchief before opening the door into the house. There was a lot of barking inside, but the listing indicated "dogs friendly" so we entered. There were dogs everywhere! They had run of the whole place and the smell was so bad I began to gag. The client who obviously had not over exaggerated his story kept a handkerchief over his face and looked at me with pity. The stench was obscene. Happy pooches jumped from couch to floor, table to chair and acted like a jolly group of kids in a playground! All the furniture was dirty, chewed and frayed.

I followed my client from one room to the next, dogs everywhere! I was feeling so traumatized, it was all I could do to keep from vomiting. I held on in the name of real estate salesmanship. At the end of the house tour, I was clinging to the back of my client's shirt when we finally stepped into the backyard for a breath of fresh air. There was a small ten by twelve shed opposite the courtyard area. When we leaned in to take a look, we discovered it to be a clean and tidy little studio apartment. That was where the owner lived. He had given his entire house over to his dogs.

My client ended up buying the house against my recommendation. I am sure his motive was to save his neighborhood from the disgusting nuisance. That is the only time in my long career I ever sold a real dog house.

Long Live Woman's Best Friend

Aaahh...the intricacies of probate sales and the idiosyncrasies of deceased owners. I have worked quite a bit in this area of real estate and there was one probate listing I had years ago that stands out in my memory.

An elderly lady passed away in the early part of 2009. Her Will stipulated that the house where she lived with her beloved dog could not be sold after her death until the dog passed away. She specified that the dog should continue to live in the house with free access in and out. The Will further required that either her son or a hired person should oversee the dog's daily care. She dictated that her beloved pooch should have a lounging sofa on the patio, and generally any other necessities to maintain the comfort of her faithful friend as long as it lived.

In early 2010, the son of the deceased lady listed the house with me due to the fact that the dog was in failing health. It had developed cancer and Alzheimer's disease. Yes, the old dog was becoming disoriented and occasionally lost in its own backyard, seemingly not able to remember the way back into the house at night. I was given very specific instructions from the son for showing the property so that the dog would not be disturbed in any way. As far as I could tell, everyone going through the house was careful to honor those instructions in consideration of the faithful old companion's last days in the home.

When we sold the property, the dog was weak but still alive. The new owner offered to keep her and continue giving her full care if the son so wished, but the decision was made to put the "Queen of the House" to sleep before we closed escrow. Long live woman's best friend.

Humane Being

This is a true story that can be documented quite easily. During my tenure as a Humane Investigator with the Department of Agriculture, animal neglect complaints seemed to be coming from the same neighborhood routinely. When responding to one particular neglect case there, I found a small dog that was dead. It was obvious it had been tied outside the owner's trailer for some time and neglected. When I issued a violation notice, I noticed in our files that the total number of cases in that trailer park, as well as the extreme nature of the cases, was inordinate. I felt something needed to be done. Since the small trailer park was outside the jurisdiction of the city police, only county law enforcement could intervene and they were slow to take action and understaffed.

To my dismay, I received yet another complaint of neglect at the same trailer park. This time when I went to investigate, I was approached by a man who asked what I was doing there. I identified myself and learned he was the park owner. I gave the owner my educational lecture on animal neglect and abuse which annoyed the guy so badly that he said, "If you're so worried about the animals, then buy the park!" I said okay and earnestly vowed to do some research on the idea. Next day I went straight to my lender to discuss loan options and wrote an offer to purchase the park. I closed on the deal Fourth of July weekend.

Every tenant was given full legal notice to vacate and I began demolition of the rat-trap trailers. The place was really hell on earth. The first day of demolition there were eleven trailers crushed and hauled away which fetched two dogs and five cats that I took to the Humane Society. The second day, all but one trailer was demolished and one more kitty was rescued, also abandoned by it former owners. There was only one trailer left and the squatter refused to leave, so I ended up in Circuit Court to have the guy finally removed.

It was a happy day finally getting rid of that eye sore of a place, both for me and the people of our community. Now that the property was cleaned up, it could be annexed to the city. Even though it cost me over $200,000 to complete the project and restore the land from the trash heap it had become, can you put a dollar value on animal suffering?

Little did I know that someone was looking over my shoulder during my mission. Was it the spirit of my first German shepherd Dutchess? Or the spirit of my first cat Tiger? Maybe it was St. Francis of Assisi! Because unbeknownst to me in the beginning, the property was located in a special planning district. A group of investors ended up purchasing the property from me for a $200,000 profit!

Real estate is a service industry that sometimes mysteriously rewards noble ambitions.

Field Of Dreams

Years ago my family vacationed in Los Angeles, California. Dad, who especially loved Beverly Hills, always wanted to live out on the West Coast and suggested to mom we should look at homes during the visit. The next thing you know, Sunday morning rolled around and a Realtor picked us up in a really fancy car. It was either a Rolls or Bentley, convertible too! She rolled out the red carpet thinking we were very serious buyers, picking us up at the Beverly Wilshire with its hoity-toity reputation and all.

Mom, dad, my little brother and I were escorted through several huge homes that day. I was mesmerized by the beauty and style of the area, especially Bel Air in the hills west of LA where one of the homes we viewed was the former home of Lucille Ball. My brother, around age ten at the time, absolutely LOVED Lucille Ball. He had watched every "I Love Lucy" show ever made and beyond that, probably watched every episode at least ten times. He really laughed at her slapstick humor. Lucy was his idol. It surprised me how my little brother relished the experience of standing in her kitchen, sitting on her bed and imagining his idol had actually lived there. His TV idol somehow became real to him that day. He was experiencing a dream come true and wiggled in his excitement. Watching him, I wondered if I would ever have an idol that would make me feel that way.

Thirty-five years later, I am a Realtor in one of the other prestigious areas of the United States, Palm Beach, Florida. It was a

Saturday morning as I was heading to the office and had a phone call in my car. I answered, "Good morning, this is Donald." The voice on the other end said, "Hi Donald, this is Henry Aaron." My heart skipped a beat. As a baseball fanatic, my hero was Hank Aaron. This couldn't be, I thought to myself. No. This had to be my broker friend who pranks me frequently by impersonating some famous person. Wait. He never knew my secret idol was Hank Aaron…

Shaking myself to focus again on the call, I piped, "THE Henry Aaron?"

"Well," he says, "I'm not sure exactly who you mean, but I did play a fair share of baseball in my time."

I was nearly speechless. My baseball hero called ME out of the blue. What a moment this was and turned out, Mr. Aaron wanted me to sell his house! He heard I had sold a home for his neighbor and got my name from him. When I went to visit Mr. Aaron that afternoon at the home, I thought about my brother thirty-five years ago visiting Lucy's house in Bel Air. I was thrilled to meet Mr. Aaron in person and did my darned best not to lose my professional composure. Deep inside I was wiggling with excitement. As he showed me around I thought, "This is Mr. Aaron's study, his living room, this is where he eats." Yes, I was feeling just like my brother felt years ago.

I asked Mr. Aaron if I could market the property as one of his personal homes. He gave permission for me to use the language, "Own the Home of Baseball's Greatest Living Legend," but seemed embarrassed that I wanted to spotlight him that way. I explained I could put a premium on the asking price by doing this and he was pleased with my plan.

The Wall Street Journal picked up the story on the listing and other newspapers followed suit. The property sold this past winter. The wonderful truth here is that I got to walk onto my Field Of Dreams. Maybe you will too!

Pay It Forward

I came to my brokerage in February 2011 from another real estate company. The listings I had came with me. Among those listings was a condominium that was the lowest priced property in my inventory. I was not the first agent to have the listing. It had been on the market for over 600 days with an original listing price of $94,999 and now reduced to $49,000. The seller was disappointed about the price, but more disappointed that it had not yet sold.

The seller was a widow in her late 70's and not in the best of health. She moved out of state to be near her son, leaving the condo vacant. The unit was in excellent condition with a neutral décor. All the appliances were original and spotlessly clean. It was a move-in ready place, and we needed a cash buyer as the complex was not FHA approved for financing.

One morning I received a call from a young woman who wanted to look at the condo. In qualifying her, I found out that she had previously viewed the property with another agent; her agent was not available to show it to her that afternoon. After contacting the other agent, working under ministerial action, I showed the property to the woman and her mother.

The next day, the buyer's agent called. She had an all cash offer for me to present to my seller. She also had a letter from the buyer explaining her circumstances and wished the letter to be presented with her offer. The letter stated she was a single mother. It detailed the fact that her husband had left her when their daughter was two years old and that her daughter was now fourteen. Proudly so, this mother told of her daughter being a straight-A student. Over the years, she and her daughter had been renting places or staying with relatives at times. The buyer put herself through college and earned a degree in Early Childhood Development. She was currently employed as director at a local childcare/preschool and studying for her master's degree. Having so many student loans, she had been unable to qualify for a home loan, however, she was making a good salary. She had been saving into a special account to purchase a place to call home. Further explaining in her letter, she said the location of this condo was perfect for she and her daughter in that it was both located in the school district that would challenge her gifted daughter and convenient to her work. Their current rental was being sold and she was now pressed to find another place to live. Finally, she commented about her low offer, her very low offer, and asked if the seller would at least consider it. Being made in good faith, she would be eternally grateful to have it considered. This young woman's letter was simply honest and beautifully written.

As my seller did not have access to a computer or fax machine, I phoned her to discuss the offer. I explained that the offer was $10,000 cash, to close in three weeks, and hoped that she would not just fall apart with disappointment, but she agreed to hear me out. I read the letter to her.

There was a long silence at the other end of the phone when I finished, and after a few moments my client in a tearful whisper began, "I was in an abusive relationship during my whole marriage. Many, many people came to my rescue over those difficult years. I was shown acts of kindness for which I am eternally grateful. Without those people and their caring, I just wouldn't have made it."

Then, without hesitation she said, "I will counter the offer at $15,000 so I don't have to bring money to the closing table. I realize any equity would have been retirement money for me, but I will sell the condo to her for $15,000 cash. I must pass on the act of kindness that was shown to me earlier in my life." By the end of the conversation, we were both in tears.

Fed-Ex picked up the contract package and all was agreed to by the buyer. Three weeks later, sitting at the closing table were the two attorneys, the buyer, her sister and myself. We were all in tears; yes, even the attorneys were emotional – for a beautiful, wonderful lady from out of state who had never met this young mother did this as an act of kindness…by paying it forward.

A Storybook Ending

It was September 2002 and I had only earned my real estate license a few weeks earlier. I had also completed the standard rookie training from Midge, our national trainer, who was conducting classes for the agency's new territory. There I was taught to wear my new Realtor name tag everywhere I went in public and that evening I wore it proudly into my local Walmart.

The greeter was a young man who I had seen there for many years. He was disabled and relied on a powered wheelchair to get around, welcoming customers with a friendly greeting. My eight year old daughter was with me so we paused at the entrance for him to put the special Walmart smiley face sticker on her hand. My shiny new Realtor badge must have caught his eye because he said, "I see you have on your name tag."

"Oh, yes. I want someone to stop me and talk about real estate!"

He sat up a little taller in his chair, then responded, "I want to talk about real estate, but nobody seems to want to talk to me."

How could I not take this opportunity to start practicing my new profession?

His name was Steve. As I would later find out, his story was a tale of sadness, perseverance and tenacity. He was born with cerebral palsy and abandoned by his single mother, left to be raised in state institutions. He was told that he could never live on his own nor hold any sort of a real job. Years later and still under the state's care, he was moved to a group home and successfully graduated from high school. He had been a greeter at Walmart for over ten years and was now living in a rented condo with one roommate through the assistance of an agency for the disabled. Whenever he told people he planned to buy a home some day, they pretty much laughed him off for such an incredulous notion. His cause became my cause.

Several Realtors told me I was wasting my time with him, but I undertook to look into his situation closer. I got the details of his finances and searched out loan programs that were available to him. There were no home buyer programs specifically designed for disabled people at that time, although there are a few today. I learned that disabled people get very little public assistance and their social security disability income is based on their work income. Steve's income was very low. This was going to be a challenge.

Steve was finally preapproved for a $56,000 loan and by then, he had saved about $7,000 from his salary. We knew that due to his disability, any home we found would have to be handicap-ready and this would take cash for the necessary renovations. Remodeling to make the bathroom accessible, widening doorways and building wheelchair ramps would be expensive, but we kept up our vigil looking for a place located close to his job. We settled on a condo unit next door to his current place. It was a FSBO. I got myself face to face with the owner and was able to negotiate an agreed price.

While the price fit Steve's loan amount, I then realized the monthly HOA fee would put him over the qualifying ratio for final approval. We were coming up short and I went into a stressful scramble the next couple of weeks. I called the Employment Security Commission to investigate Steve's benefits. During one of those calls I heard a faint gasp from the woman on the other end of the phone. An error had been made. Turns out that Steve should have been elevated to a higher benefit years before. Several weeks later his SSDI was not only increased but he received a lump sum back payment. He would be able to buy his own place.

During the sixteen months that I worked on Steve's cause, I suffered a heart attack. In short time I made a full recovery and was able to push for the final challenges of my friend's purchase and move. I found a contractor who single-handedly made the handicap modifications to the condo. I was able to do much of the painting myself and organized a group of volunteers from my Sunday school class to help. We received assistance from a disability group in town called ARC, and even the seller of the condo donated money for a refrigerator.

For the Realtors who said I was wasting my time, this is what I got out of the deal. I gained valuable experience as a rookie agent by going through the transaction process from start to finish. I formed a solid business relationship with the loan officer who was so kind to us. I learned about funding for low income and disabled people. There was a feature article in my local newspaper's home section about us. The article was also published in "REALTOR Magazine." I had changed to a different brokerage by the time the deal closed and was given a free trip to their international convention in Orlando, Florida that year, being recognized on stage at the event. I sold two other homes as a direct result of this transaction, one of which was to a couple who were both legally blind with two children - that's another amazing story. But most importantly, I gained a friend for life in Steve.

However, the next episode of this story brought yet another battle for us to face. Steve's condo was destroyed in a fire on about July 20, 2010. The fire started in the unit above his; he lost everything. Although he had taken out contents insurance when he bought the place, he had let the policy lapse. Thank goodness the HOA stepped in to help, going above and beyond the call of duty. They rebuilt his unit and even added some extra accessible features he did not have before. He is slowly replacing his contents and resuming his life, and I am continuing to help him through this transition. His cause is my cause because Steve is my friend.

The Curtain Rod

Here's a story that was submitted to me anonymously: I don't know whether it's fact or fiction, but either way, it is an unbelievable tale:

A recently divorced woman had to give up her home and all its furnishings as part of her divorce settlement. She packed up all her personal belongings into boxes, garment bags and suitcases. She then proceeded to sit down for a farewell meal in what had once been her happy home. She put candles on the dining room table, soft music on the CD player, and laid out a feast of shrimp, caviar and champagne to celebrate her new life ahead.

When she had finished, she walked around her home for one last time. She went into each and every room and focused on the happy memories. She then deposited the half eaten shrimp shells, dipped in caviar, into the hollow of the curtain rods in several of the rooms. She cleaned up the remainder of her meal, finished putting her belongings into her SUV and left.

The next day, her ex-husband and his new girlfriend moved into the home. All was bliss for the first few days. Then slowly, the house began to smell. They tried everything: cleaning and mopping and airing the place out. Vents were checked for dead rodents, and carpets were steam-cleaned. Air fresheners were hung in every room. They moved out for a few days while exterminators set off gas canisters. They replaced the expensive wool carpeting. Nothing worked.

People stopped coming over to visit. Repairmen refused to work in the house. The maid quit. Finally, they could not take the stench any longer and decided to sell the house. They listed the home with a local real estate agent.

A month later, and after several price reductions, a buyer could not be found for this stinky house. Even the real estate agent quit. Finally, they decided to move to another home across town, and had to borrow a huge amount of money for a new mortgage.

The ex-wife called her ex-husband and asked how things were going. He told her the saga of the smelly house. She listened politely and said that she missed her old home terribly and would be willing to buy the house, even though it obviously had some kind of a problem. Knowing his ex-wife had no idea how bad the smell was, he agreed on a price that was a 10th of what the house had been worth-but only if she were to sign the papers that very day. She agreed, and within the hour, his lawyers delivered the paperwork.

A week later, the man and his new girlfriend stood smirking as they watched the moving company pack everything to take to their new home….including the curtain rods.

The Author's Story

Real Estate's "Other" Donald

Donald Gorbach is believed to be the youngest agent who ever listed and sold a house at the age of twelve. It was his best friend's home and Donald convinced his friend's parents to list with his

The Author's Story

dad's real estate company. Then one snowy day when the open house was cancelled due to weather, Donald's father told him to sit at the house that was just down the street. His instructions were simple, "If anyone shows up, just take them through the house and have them call me with any questions." Sure enough, a couple showed up, loved the home and bought it the next day. Donald was addicted to real estate ever since, although he is still waiting for his commission check.

Donald is a graduate of Vanderbilt University and sells luxury real estate in Palm Beach, Florida. He is the principal owner of YHD Realty, specializing in luxury oceanfront condominiums in the southern Palm Beach area. Although Donald has been telling real estate stories for years and collecting them from agents all over the country, this is his first time sharing his favorites in literary form. He hopes you enjoy them as much as he has enjoyed bringing them to you.

CONTRIBUTOR LIST

The Greatest Stories from The Greatest Agents
(*multiple great stories)

ADELMAN, Barry	Find Your Austin	Austin TX
ALLEN, Dennis	Astick Realty	Brigantine NJ
ALLISON, Birgit	Allison & Associates	Charlotte NC
ALLISON, Tiffany	Corcoran Group	Palm Beach FL
ANGLIN, Brigit	Coldwell Banker	Vista CA
ASBURY, Christina	Exit/Independence Rlty	Jacksonville NC
BELL, Jenny	The Negotiators Realty	Tucson AZ
BENOIT, Randy	The Franklin Group	Kaysville UT
BERNADSKY, Mike	ERA Henley Real Estate	Conway AR
BLETSH, Rhonda	Independent Agent	Conway AR
BLUMBERG, Paul	Howard Hanna	Pepper Pike OH
BROWN, Flavia	The Real Estate Group	Torrance CA
BROWNYARD, Brooke	Re/Max of the Islands	Sanibel FL
BURR, Patricia	Realty One Group	Las Vegas NV
COMER, Todd*	Advantage Residential	Charlotte NC
COSTEN, Josephine	Century 21 Alliance	Forth Worth TX
COULTER, Becky	Century 21 Award	San Diego CA
COVAN, Art & Lynn	Re/Max Associates	Columbus OH
CUTLER, Jonathan	Frank Howard Allen Realtors	Greenbrae CA
DaCOSTA, Juliana*	Juliana DaCosta Realty	Fort Meyers FL

Contributor List

ELGART, Sheila	Prudential California Realty	Cucamonga CA
ELLIS, Susan	Nextage Sonoran Realty	Scottsdale AZ
FACCI, Lynda	Scott Gordon Realty	Palm Beach FL
FARISCHON, Nancy Barg	Coldwell Banker	Lake Ridge VA
FELDMAN, Rick	R&R Property Mgmt	Chatsworth CA
FITZPATRICK, Dick*	Fitzpatrick School of R.E.	Palm Beach Gardens FL
FLYE, Celeste	Coldwell Banker	Las Vegas NV
FOLEY, Jeremiah	Independent Agent	Los Angeles CA
FOX, Cheryl	Properties Plus	Encino CA
GRAFF, Judy	John Aaroe Group	Los Angeles CA
GULLO, Tom & Arlene	Corcoran Group	Palm Beach FL
HATCH, Barbara	Troop Real Estate	Camarillo CA
HATZFIELD, Larry	Avalar Austin Real Estate	Austin TX
HERKNER, Lynda	Century 21 Northland	Traverse City MI
HESSE, Karin	Peninsula Properties	Tampa FL
JONES, Kathryn	Alfa Realty	Montgomery AL
KITER, Vera	Manatee Cove Realty	Lake Worth FL
LANE, Rose	Rose Lane Broker	Westlake Village CA
LEAL, Kimberly	Keller Williams Realty	Campbell CA
LEGAN, David	Diamond Realty	Bossier City VA
LEVESQUE, Irene	Century 21	Wrentham MA
LEWI, Peter	Masterpiece Realty Assoc.	Del Mar CA
LUGER, Sylvia	Independent Agent	Boca Raton FL

READY, WILLING & (unbeliev)ABLE

LURIE, Richard*	RL Custom Real Estate Emails	Denver CO
MANN, Jonathan	Corcoran Group	Palm Beach FL
MARKS, Lance	Rodeo Realty	Calabasas CA
McCORMICK, Ivona	@ Properties	Evanston IL
MEDARIS, John	Exit/ Advantage	Fairfax VA
MENASKANIAN, "Vic"	Independent Agent	Alabama
MEYERS, Joana	East Oahu Realty	Honolulu HI
MILLER, Ed	Century 21 Advantage	Philadelphia PA
MONSOUR, Karen	Coldwell Banker	Fort Lauderdale FL
NEWKIRK, Ralph	Real Estate One	Southfield MI
PEPPER, Carl	Tierra Antigua Realty	Tucson AZ
PEREZ, Dennis	Realcom Associates	Santa Clara CA.
SEFTON, Chandra*	Baird & Warner	Libertyville IL
SEVERINO, David	Severino Real Estate	Normal IL
SHEBROE, Jane	Better Homes Realty	Montclair NJ
STAPP, Donald Lee	Realty Associates	Houston TX
STEPPENBACKER, Sandy	Re/Max Beyond 2000	Middlebury Hts. OH
SUPNICK, Darlene	Realty Mark Professionals	Cherry Hill NJ
UMBENHAUER, Todd	Keller Williams Realty	Montgomeryville PA
VASILOPULOS, Marilyn	Baird & Warner	Olympia Fields IL
VELASQUEZ, Maria	Rodeo Realty	Sherman Oaks CA
WARD, Scott	Exit/Reward Realty	Pittsfield NH
WEBB, Terry	Street Sotheby's Int'l Realty	Columbus OH

Contributor List

WEEGMANN, Jennie	Bob Parks Realty	Murfreesboro TN
WICKHAM, Jeanne	Independent Agent	New Albany OH
WINDER, Jerome	Prudential Gardner Realtors	New Orleans LA
WILSON, Gary	Wilson Properties	Corralitos CA
YAHN, William*	Corcoran Group	Palm Beach FL

Made in the USA
Middletown, DE
11 December 2019